I can Grammar 4

지은이

신석영
現 아일랜드 교육 대표
Just Reading HR 1, 2, 3 (전 3권)
Just Grammar 1, 2, 3 A / 1, 2, 3 B (전 6권)
Aim Higher English Skills for Assessment (전 3권)
Voca Killer (전 3권)

감수

김상민
現 에이플러스 최강영어 대표

I can Grammar Book 4

지은이	신석영
펴낸이	신성현, 오상욱
관리	허윤정
펴낸곳	도서출판 아이엠북스
	(153-802) 서울시 금천구 가산동 327-32 대륭테크노타운 12차 1116호
대표전화	02-6343-0999
팩스	02-6343-0995
출판등록	2006년 6월 7일
	제 313-2006-000122호
ISBN	978-89-92334-87-7 64740

www.iambooks.co.kr

I can Grammar 4

Iam books

문법은 반드시 필요한 학습이지만,
올바른 학습 방법이 아니면 의미가 없습니다

이제는 영어를 통해 전 세계와 의사소통을 하고, 학문과 지식을 습득하는 세계인이 되기 위해서는 필수적으로 갖추어야 할 가장 기본적인 도구중 하나가 바로 영어라고 해도 과언이 아닐 것입니다.

문법은 모국어를 기반으로 하지 않는 사람이 외국어를 공부할 때 반드시 그 기본체계를 익혀야 하는 중요한 학습입니다. 요즘에는 "문법 무용론"을 주장하는 사람들도 있지만, 이는 우리나라의 영어 교육 환경이 EFL(English as a Foreign Language) 환경임을 제대로 이해하지 못하는 발상에서 나오는 잘못된 생각입니다. 이미 초등학생으로 성장한 우리 아이들이 영어를 모국어로 자연스럽게 체득이 될 수 있는 단계가 지나버린 즉, "외국어로서의 언어"를 공부해야 하는 상황을 이해한다는 올바른 문법 교육이 그 어느 때보다 더 절실한 때입니다.

그동안의 우리 주변에 있는 문법책들을 살펴보면, **1** 품사 위주의 문법 번역식 교재 **2** EFL 환경을 무시한 원서 교재 **3** 한국 초등학생들에게 적합하지 않은 무분별한 원서 교재

마지막으로 올바른 학습법 보다는 중요도의 구분이 없고, 복잡한 문법 학습 체계로 초등학생에게는 너무나도 생소한 용어와 크게 중요하지도 않은 문법 사항들을 강조, 나열함으로써 중학교에 입학하기도 전에 영어를 포기하게 되거나, 문법에 대한 거부감, 학습 장애를 초래하는 결과를 낳기도 했습니다.

누구나 다 문법을 공부하지만 아무나 올바른 방법으로 공부하지 못합니다

영어를 필요에 의해서만 공부했지, "올바른" 학습 방법으로 공부를 하지 못한다는 것이 가장 큰 문제점이였습니다. I can Grammar는 저자가 수년간 현장 교육에서 오랜 세월동안 직접 가르치며 만들었습니다. 아이들과 함께, 울고, 웃고, 기뻐하며 힘들고 행복했던 시간들을 함께 하면서 조금씩 다듬어 나갔습니다. 이제 이 땅에서 우리 아이들이 더 이상 영어로 인해 힘들어 하지 않고 영어 학습이 가장 자랑스럽고, 자신감 있는 아이들로 만들어 줄 I can Grammar를 가만히 내놓습니다.

Preface

문법 교육에 있어 "재미와 흥미"를 이끌어 줄 수 있는 교재가 절실히 필요하다

독해나 다른 영역도 마찬가지겠지만 특히 문법 교육에 있어서는 "어떤 교재로 가르치느냐?", "그 교재가 아이들의 흥미와 재미를 유발할 수 있는가?"하는 것은 굉장히 중요한 사항입니다. 영어 실력도 중요하지만 무엇보다도 아이들의 특성을 이해하고 인지 발달 단계와 언어 학습 원리에 맞게 정말 재미있는 교재가 필요합니다. I can Grammar는 핵심 문법 개념을 재미있는 그림과 삽화를 통해 수업 자체가 재미있도록 구성하였고, 영문법의 중요 개념을 재미있고 체계적으로 이해하고 익힐 수 있도록 기획되었습니다. 특히 예문들이 실용적인 유용한 표현들이어서 영어의 형태, 의미, 주요 회화표현까지도 익힐 수 있는 교재입니다.

배우기도 쉽고, 가르치기도 가장 편한 교재!

학생 스스로 예습 및 복습이 가능하도록 정밀히 고안된 독창적인 장치들로 구성이 되었고, 자세한 설명과 예문, 그리고 배운 내용을 바로 바로 확인 할 수 있는 단계별 누적 문제 시스템이 적용되어 차례대로 학습만 하면 저절로 복습되도록 기획 되었습니다.

또한 선생님들은 풍부한 단계별 문제와 심화, 발전, Writing 영역까지 고루 학습 장치가 마련되어 수업하기도, 확인학습도, 그리고 숙제 내주기도 가장 편한 교재입니다.

마지막으로 학습 효과를 극대화하기 위한 5단계 누적 실전 훈련 시스템으로 기본 단계에서 발전, 심화 단계까지 아이들의 이해정도를 바로바로 확인하고 보완해 줄 수 있는 최적의 교재가 되어 줄 것입니다.

I can Grammar가 출간되기까지 더 좋은 책을 위해 최선을 다해주신 iambooks 관계자 여러분들께 깊은 감사를 드립니다. 마지막으로 힘들고 지칠 때 언제나 뒤에서 힘이 되어준 내 아내 미선이, 딸 서윤이에게 감사와 사랑을 전합니다.

2009년 6월 신석영

I can Grammar는 학생 스스로 예습 및 복습이 가능하도록 정밀히 고안된 독창적인 장치들로 구성이 되었고, 자세한 설명과 예문, 그리고 배운 내용을 바로 바로 확인 할 수 있는 단계별 누적 문제 시스템이 적용되어 차례대로 학습만 하면 저절로 복습되도록 기획되었습니다.

TARGET WORDS 각 Unit은 학습 내용과 관련된 핵심 단어들을 확인해보는 것으로 시작합니다. 알고 있는 단어는 다시 확인하고 넘어가고 몰랐던 단어는 익히고 넘어갈 수 있도록 하였습니다.

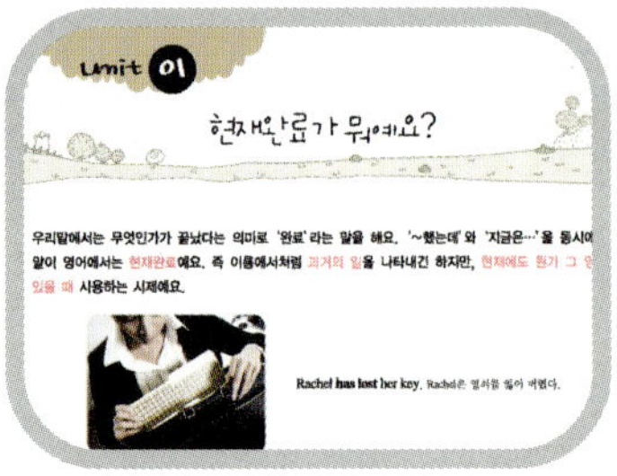

Grammar Points 중요한 핵심 문법 용어와 개념을 여러 가지 예문과 사진 그리고 삽화를 통해 쉽게 이해 할 수 있도록 설명하고 있습니다.

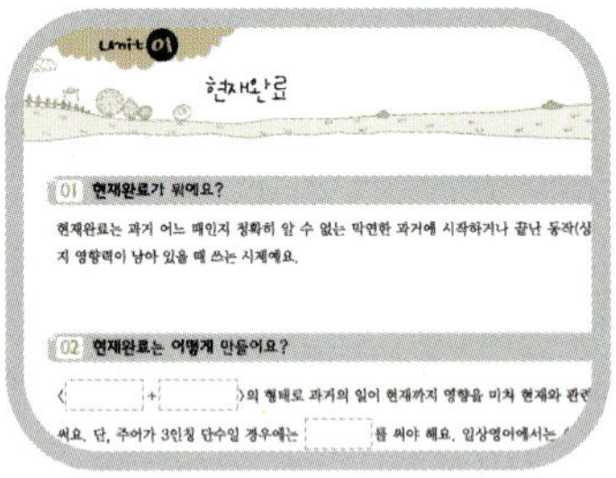

Mini Test 본격적으로 문제를 풀어보기 전에, 앞서 배운 핵심 문법 사항과 규칙을 잘 이해했는지 간단한 테스트를 통해 한 번 더 정리 해 볼 수 있도록 하였습니다.

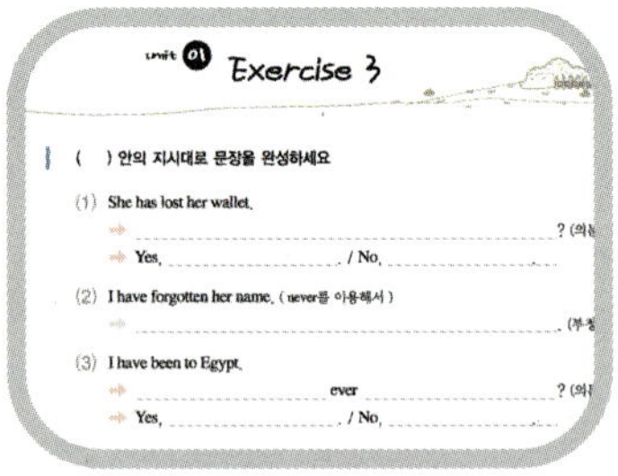

Exercise 1, 2, 3 다양한 형태로 제시되는 문제들을 통해 문법 개념을 확실히 이해하고 실력을 굳힐 수 있도록 하였습니다.

Structures & Features

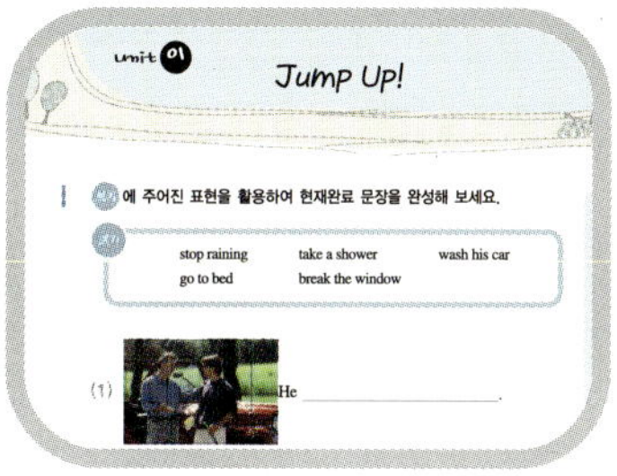
unit 01 Jump Up!

1 에 주어진 표현을 활용하여 현재완료 문장을 완성해 보세요.

stop raining / take a shower / wash his car / go to bed / break the window

(1) He ______________.

Jump Up! 앞에서 배운 문법 사항과 규칙을 이용한 고난이도 문법 문제를 풀어보며 자신의 실력을 향상시킬 수 있도록 구성하였습니다.

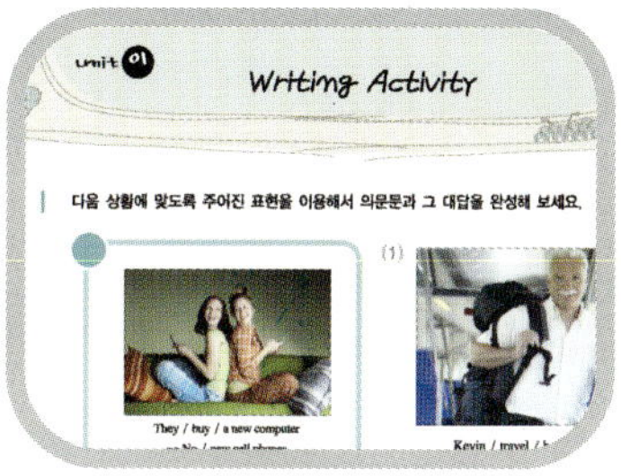
unit 01 Writing Activity

1 다음 상황에 맞도록 주어진 표현을 이용해서 의문문과 그 대답을 완성해 보세요.

They / buy / a new computer

(1) Kevin / travel / ...

Writing Activity 앞서 배운 문법이 영작문 실력의 향상으로 이어질 수 있도록 직접 문장 안에 넣어보고 써보는 서술형 문제로 구성하였습니다.

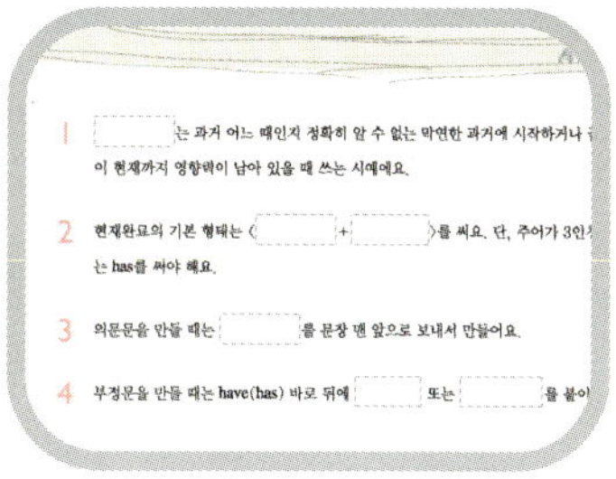
1 ______는 과거 어느 때인지 정확히 알 수 없는 막연한 과거에 시작하거나 ...
이 현재까지 영향력이 남아 있을 때 쓰는 시제에요.

2 현재완료의 기본 형태는 (______ + ______)를 써요. 단, 주어가 3인칭 ...
는 has를 써야 해요.

3 의문문을 만들 때는 ______를 문장 맨 앞으로 보내서 만들어요.

4 부정문을 만들 때는 have(has) 바로 뒤에 ______ 또는 ______를 붙이 ...

Oral Test! 앞서 배운 문법과 단어들을 소리 내어 다시 복습해 볼 수 있도록 하였습니다.

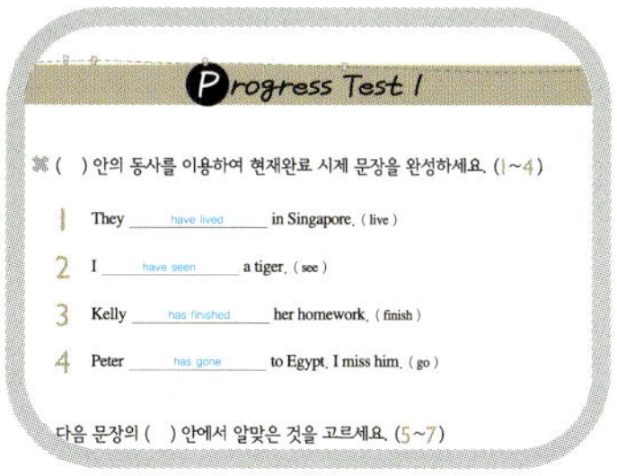
Progress Test 1

※ ( ) 안의 동사를 이용하여 현재완료 시제 문장을 완성하세요. (1~4)

1 They ___have lived___ in Singapore. (live)

2 I ___have seen___ a tiger. (see)

3 Kelly ___has finished___ her homework. (finish)

4 Peter ___has gone___ to Egypt. I miss him. (go)

다음 문장의 ( ) 안에서 알맞은 것을 고르세요. (5~7)

Progress Test 3~5개의 Unit이 끝날 때마다 Progress Test를 통해 배운 문법을 복습해보고 다시 정리 해 보도록 하였습니다.

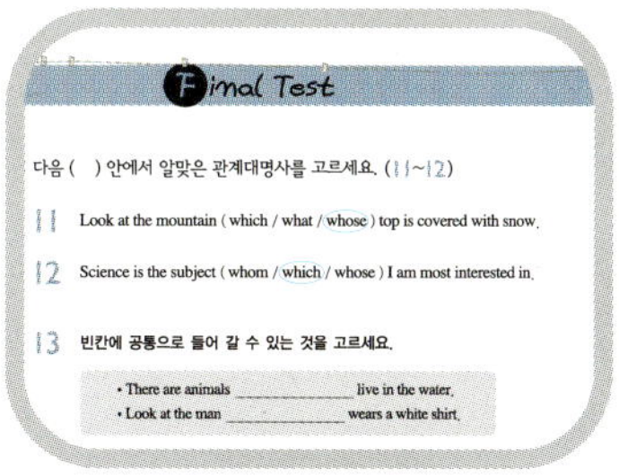
Final Test

다음 ( ) 안에서 알맞은 관계대명사를 고르세요. (11~12)

11 Look at the mountain (which / what / whose) top is covered with snow.

12 Science is the subject (whom / which / whose) I am most interested in.

13 빈칸에 공통으로 들어 갈 수 있는 것을 고르세요.

• There are animals ____________ live in the water.
• Look at the man ____________ wears a white shirt.

Final Test 한 권을 마무리하며 이제껏 배운 내용을 중심으로 종합평가를 풀어보면서 배운 문법 사항을 마무리 할 수 있도록 하였습니다.

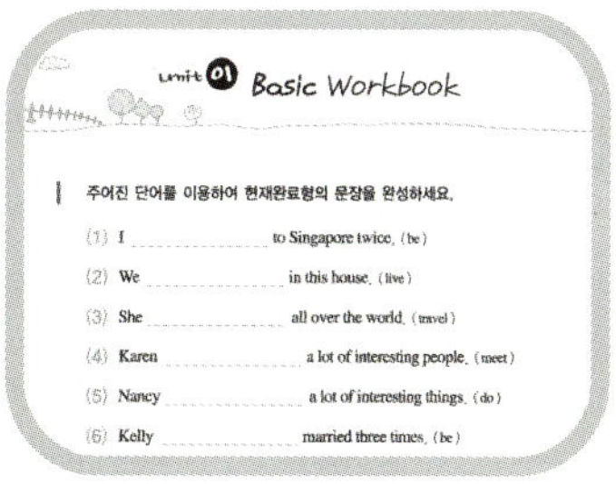
unit 01 Basic Workbook

1 주어진 단어를 이용하여 현재완료형의 문장을 완성하세요.

(1) I ____________ to Singapore twice. (be)
(2) We ____________ in this house. (live)
(3) She ____________ all over the world. (travel)
(4) Karen ____________ a lot of interesting people. (meet)
(5) Nancy ____________ a lot of interesting things. (do)
(6) Kelly ____________ married three times. (be)

Workbook(Basic Workbook, Practice Workbook) 별책으로 들어있는 Workbook은 매 unit마다 좀 더 다양하고 더 많은 연습문제들을 접해봄으로써 문법 사항을 확실하게 익힐 수 있도록 하였습니다.

Contents

I can Grammar series

Book 1

Book 2

Book 3

Book 4

Unit 01

현재완료

TARGET WORDS 알고 있는 단어는 check(√) 후 뜻을 쓰고, 모르는 단어는 조사해 오세요!

- ☐ lose ⓥ ______
- ☐ already ⓐⓓ ______
- ☐ wine ⓝ ______
- ☐ movie theater ______
- ☐ wallet ⓝ ______
- ☐ take a shower ______
- ☐ go to bed ______
- ☐ windsurfing ⓝ ______
- ☐ leg ⓝ ______
- ☐ complete ⓥ ______
- ☐ snake ⓝ ______
- ☐ prepare ⓥ ______
- ☐ Egypt ⓝ ______
- ☐ wash a car ______
- ☐ travel ⓥ ______
- ☐ museum ⓝ ______
- ☐ taste ⓥ ______
- ☐ zoo ⓝ ______
- ☐ ride ⓥ ______
- ☐ yet ⓐⓓ ______
- ☐ break ⓥ ______
- ☐ horse ⓝ ______

Unit 01

현재완료가 뭐예요?

우리말에서는 무엇인가가 끝났다는 의미로 '완료'라는 말을 해요. '~했는데'와 '지금은…'을 동시에 나타내주는 말이 영어에서는 현재완료예요. 즉 이름에서처럼 과거의 일을 나타내긴 하지만, 현재에도 뭔가 그 영향력이 남아 있을 때 사용하는 시제예요.

Rachel **has lost** her key. Rachel은 열쇠를 잃어 버렸다.

Rachel은 열쇠를 지금 찾고 있지만 찾을 수가 없네요. Rachel은 과거 어느 때인가 열쇠를 잃어버렸고 지금은 그 열쇠가 없다는 것을 함께 표현해 주는 시제가 현재완료 시제예요.

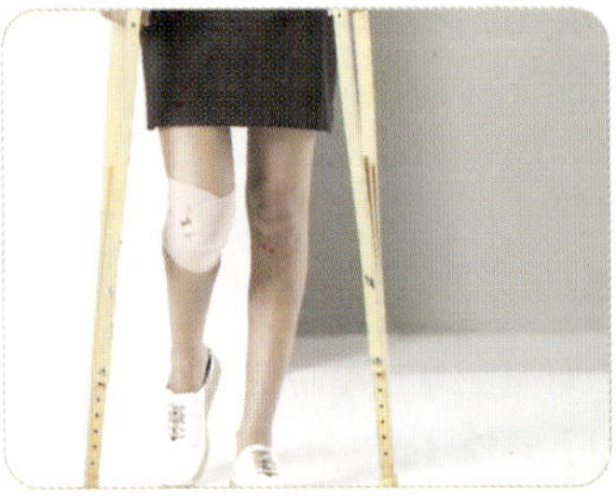

I **have broken** my leg. 나는 다리가 부러졌다.

현재완료는 이미 과거에 끝난 일이지만 현재와 연결되어 그 동작이나 상태가 현재까지 이어져 있음을 나타내요. 현재도 다리가 부러져 있다는 사실에 관심을 두고 이야기하는 거예요.

현재완료는 언제 다리가 부러졌는지에 대한 특정한 시간이 중요하지 않다는 것을 기억하세요. 정확히 언제 그랬는지에 대한 특정한 과거의 시간을 언급하려면 과거 시제를 써야 해요.

보통 일상영어에서는 〈주어' ve(주어's) + -ed〉로 줄여 써요.

자! 그러면 현재완료 시제를 만드는 방법을 알아볼까요?

현재완료 시제는 언제나 〈have(has)+-ed〉의 형태로 만들어요. 동사를 -ed나 -en의 형태(과거분사)로 만들고 앞에는 항상 have(has)를 붙여주면 돼요.

하나, be동사가 있을 때는 be동사를 been으로 고쳐 〈have(has)+been〉으로 만들면 간단해요.

We **have been** good friends. 우리는 좋은 친구 사이야.
(과거에도 친구 ——————➤ 지금도 계속 친구 사이)

둘, 일반동사일 때는, 일반동사에 -ed를 붙여 〈have(has)+-ed〉로 만들면 돼요.

I **have finished** my homework. 나는 숙제를 다 했다.
(과거 어느 때 시작 ——————➤ 지금은 끝났다)

그럼 이번에는 현재완료의 의문문과 부정문 만드는 방법에 대해서도 알아보아요.
부정문을 만들려면 not 또는 nerer를 have(has) 뒤에 붙이면 돼요.
의문문을 만들려면 have(has)를 문장의 맨 앞으로 보내고 문장 뒤에 물음표(?)를 붙이면 돼요.

She **has studied** English. 그녀는 영어 공부를 했다.
부정문 ➜ She **has not studied** (hasn't studied) English. 그녀는 영어 공부를 하지 않았다.
의문문 ➜ **Has** she **studied** English? 그녀는 영어 공부를 했나요?
Yes, she **has**. / No, she **hasn't**. (대답은 완료 시제에 쓰인 have(has)를 이용해요.)

Alice **has gone** to the museum. Alice는 박물관에 갔다.
부정문 ➜ Alice **has not gone** (hasn't gone) to the museum. Alice는 박물관에 가지 않았다.
의문문 ➜ **Has** Alice **gone** to the museum? Alice는 박물관에 갔나요?
Yes, she **has**. / No, she **hasn't**.

보통 일상영어에서는 〈haven't/hasn't+-ed〉로 줄여 써요.

Unit 01

현재완료

01 **현재완료**가 뭐예요?

현재완료는 과거 어느 때인지 정확히 알 수 없는 막연한 과거에 시작하거나 끝난 동작(상태)이 현재까지 영향력이 남아 있을 때 쓰는 시제예요.

02 **현재완료**는 **어떻게** 만들어요?

〈 ______ + ______ 〉의 형태로 과거의 일이 현재까지 영향을 미쳐 현재와 관련 있는 경우에 써요. 단, 주어가 3인칭 단수일 경우에는 ______ 를 써야 해요. 일상영어에서는 〈주어've(주어's)+과거분사〉로 줄여 써요.

I **have** already **completed** my work. 나는 이미 내 일을 끝냈다.
I **have seen** a ghost before. 나는 전에 귀신을 본 적이 있다.

03 **의문문**은 **어떻게** 만들어요?

______ 를 문장 맨 앞에 보내고 문장 끝에 물음표(?)를 붙여서 만들어요.

Have you **met** Nancy? 너는 Nancy를 만난 적이 있니?
➜ Yes, I **have**. 응, 그래. / No, I **haven't**. 아니, 그렇지 않아.

04 **부정문**은 **어떻게** 만들어요?

have(has) 바로 뒤에 ______ 또는 ______ 를 붙이기만 하면 돼요.

I **have not tasted** this wine. 나는 이 와인을 맛 본 적이 없다.
He **has not been** kind to her. 그는 그녀에게 친절하게 대하지 않았다.
We **have never seen** the big hamburger. 우리는 그 큰 햄버거를 본 적이 없다.

unit 01

Exercise 1

1 보기 와 같이 과거와 현재완료가 되도록 빈칸에 알맞은 과거분사형을 쓰세요.

> 보기
> went(과거) → have gone(현재완료)

(1) tried → have ______________   (2) lost → have ______________

(3) lived → have ______________   (4) was → have ______________

(5) worked → have ______________   (6) told → have ______________

(7) heard → have ______________   (8) studied → have ______________

(9) slept → have ______________   (10) visited → have ______________

(11) saw → have ______________   (12) knew → have ______________

(13) did → have ______________   (14) ate → have ______________

2 (   ) 안의 동사를 이용하여 현재완료 시제 문장을 완성하세요.

(1) They ______________________ in Korea. (live)

(2) I ______________________ a snake. (see)

(3) Peter ______________________ his work. (finish)

(4) Jane ______________________ to New York. I miss her. (go)

(5) The child ______________________ his favorite toy. (lose)

(6) We ______________________ a new car. (buy)

(7) I ______________________ of the story before. (hear)

Unit 01 Exercise 2

1 주어진 문장을 의문문으로 고쳐 쓰세요.

(1) He has washed his car.

➡ ______________________________?

(2) I have been to the zoo.

➡ ______________________________?

(3) They have seen the movie before.

➡ ______________________________?

(4) Tom has lived in Seoul.

➡ ______________________________?

(5) Kelly has been to the movie theater.

➡ ______________________________?

2 주어진 문장을 부정문으로 고쳐 쓰세요.

(1) I have prepared for the party.

➡ ______________________________.

(2) I have ridden a horse. (never를 이용해서)

➡ ______________________________.

(3) She has already finished breakfast.

➡ ______________________________ yet.

unit 01

Exercise 3

1 ( ) 안의 지시대로 문장을 완성하세요

(1) She has lost her wallet.

➡ ______________________________? (의문문)

➡ Yes, ______________. / No, ______________.

(2) I have forgotten her name. (never를 이용해서)

➡ ______________________________. (부정문)

(3) I have been to Egypt.

➡ ______________ ever ______________? (의문문)

➡ Yes, ______________. / No, ______________.

(4) Linda has already cleaned her room.

➡ ______________________________ yet. (부정문)

(5) Ron has been to Thailand.

➡ ______________________________. (부정문)

➡ ______________________________? (의문문)

2 현재완료 시제를 이용하여 완전한 문장으로 만드세요.

(1) I / leave my cellphone / in the subway

➡ ______________________________.

(2) Maria / not arrive at / the City Hall / yet

➡ ______________________________.

(3) Linda / not finish / taking a shower / yet

➡ ______________________________.

Unit 01

Jump Up!

보기 에 주어진 표현을 활용하여 현재완료 문장을 완성해 보세요.

보기

stop raining	take a shower	wash his car
go to bed	break the window	

(1)  He ________________________.

(2)  They ________________________.

(3)  It ________________________.

(4)  Somebody ________________________.

(5)  Susan ________________________.

take a shower 샤워하다
wash one's car 세차하다
break ⓥ 깨다, 부수다
go to bed 자러가다

Writing Activity

다음 상황에 맞도록 주어진 표현을 이용해서 의문문과 그 대답을 완성해 보세요.

보기

They / buy / new computers
→ No / new cellphones

Have they bought new computers?
→ No, they haven't.
They have bought new cellphones.

(1)

Kevin / travel / by airplane
→ No / by train

____________________?
→ No, __________.
He ________________.

(2)

Rachel / ever / ride / a horse
→ Yes

____________________?
→ Yes, __________.

(3)

Robert / ever / try / bungee-jumping
→ No / windsurfing

____________________?
→ No, __________.
He ________________.

unit 01

Oral Test!

1 [　　　　]는 과거 어느 때인지 정확히 알 수 없는 막연한 과거에 시작하거나 끝난 동작(상태)이 현재까지 영향력이 남아 있을 때 쓰는 시제예요.

2 현재완료의 기본 형태는 〈[　　　　] + [　　　　]〉를 써요. 단, 주어가 3인칭 단수일 경우에는 [　　　　]를 써야 해요.

3 의문문을 만들 때는 [　　　　]를 문장 맨 앞으로 보내서 만들어요.

4 부정문을 만들 때는 have(has) 바로 뒤에 [　　　　] 또는 [　　　　]를 붙이기만 하면 돼요.

REVIEW TARGET WORDS 주어진 단어의 철자/뜻을 쓰세요.

☐ ________	ⓥ 잃다	☐ leg	ⓝ ________
☐ ________	ⓝ 박물관	☐ already	ⓐⓓ ________
☐ ________	ⓥ 마치다, 끝내다	☐ taste	ⓥ ________
☐ ________	ⓝ 와인[포도주]	☐ snake	ⓝ ________
☐ ________	ⓝ 동물원	☐ movie theater	________
☐ ________	ⓥ 준비하다	☐ ride	ⓥ ________
☐ ________	ⓝ 지갑	☐ Egypt	ⓝ ________
☐ ________	ⓐⓓ (부정문에서) 아직	☐ take a shower	________
☐ ________	세차하다	☐ break	ⓥ ________
☐ ________	자러가다	☐ travel	ⓥ ________
☐ ________	ⓝ 말	☐ windsurfing	ⓝ ________

Unit 02

현재분사/과거분사

TARGET WORDS 알고 있는 단어는 check(√) 후 뜻을 쓰고, 모르는 단어는 조사해 오세요!

☐ cry	ⓥ	______	☐ break	ⓥ	______	☐ frighten	ⓥ	______
☐ bore	ⓥ	______	☐ shock	ⓥ	______	☐ hat	ⓝ	______
☐ wear	ⓥ	______	☐ product	ⓝ	______	☐ recycle	ⓥ	______
☐ machine	ⓝ	______	☐ properly	(ad)	______	☐ bark	ⓥ	______
☐ seldom	(ad)	______	☐ bite	ⓥ	______	☐ garage sale		______
☐ injure	ⓥ	______	☐ traffic accident		______	☐ noodle	ⓝ	______
☐ novel	ⓝ	______	☐ fry	ⓥ	______	☐ look for		______
☐ be filled with		______	☐ freeze	ⓥ	______	☐ vase	ⓝ	______
☐ floor	ⓝ	______	☐ popular	ⓐ	______	☐ display	ⓥ	______
☐ twinkle	ⓥ	______	☐ disappoint	ⓥ	______	☐ dangerous	ⓐ	______

Unit 02

현재분사, 과거분사가 뭐예요?

영어에서 형용사는 '명사를 꾸며주거나 설명해주는 말'이라고 배웠어요. 하지만 형용사는 pretty baby에서 pretty(예쁜)처럼 명사의 상태만을 설명해 줄 뿐 명사의 동작을 표현할 수 없어요. 그렇다고 우리말로 '울다 아기'라고 말하면 어색하겠죠? 그래서 '울고 있는 아기'처럼 '아기'라는 명사의 동작이나 행위를 표현해 주는 말(울고 있는)이 영어에서는 분사예요. 당연히 동사에서 나왔으니, 동사에 -ing를 붙인 현재분사를 써서 'crying baby(울고 있는 아기)'로 만드는 거예요.

Look at the **crying** *baby*.
울고 있는 아기를 보아라.

The baby is **crying**.
그 아기는 울고 있다.
(be+ing는 진행형이지만 crying은 단독으로 현재분사라고 해요.)

분사는 형용사와 마찬가지로 명사 앞이나 be동사 뒤에 위치해서 명사를 설명해 주는 역할을 해요. 단, 형용사와 다른 점은 분사는 명사의 동작이나 행위를 표현해 준다는 점이에요.

There is a **running** *woman*.
뛰고 있는 여자가 있다.

The woman **running** over there is my mother.
저기에서 달리고 있는 여자 분은 우리 엄마야.

현재분사 뒤에 명사를 수식해 주는 말이 여러 개 더 있을 경우, 명사 뒤에서 명사의 동작을 표현해 줘요. 명사가 직접적인 행위를 하는 주인으로 우리말 '~하는, ~하고 있는, ~하는 중인'의 뜻이 돼요.

동사에 -ing를 붙여 현재분사를 만든다는 것을 알겠죠? 동사에 -ed형태를 붙여 만드는 과거분사도 형용사처럼 명사를 설명해주는 역할을 해요. 마찬가지로 be동사 뒤에 그리고 한 단어일 때 명사 앞에 와서 명사의 행위나 동작을 표현해 주는 역할을 해요. 하지만 현재분사와 다른 점은 명사가 직접 행동을 하는 주인이 아니라 명사가 행동을 당한다는 뜻으로 '~되어진, ~해진'의 의미로 쓰여요.

Kathy found her **stolen** purse.
Kathy는 그녀의 도둑맞은 핸드백을 찾았다.

Her purse was **stolen**.
그녀의 핸드백은 도난당했었다.
(be동사 뒤에 와서 명사가 행동을 당한 상태를 표현)

과거분사도 마찬가지로 과거분사와 함께 명사를 꾸며주는 말이 몇 개 더 따라올 경우 명사 뒤에서 꾸며줘요.

Sunny is an easily **frightened** *person*.
Sunny는 쉽게 놀라는 사람이다.

The woman **frightened** by the dog is Sunny.
개에 놀란 여자는 Sunny이다.

감정을 나타내는 동사로 현재분사나 과거분사를 만들 경우 -ing는 언제나 감정을 주는 중심이 되고 -ed는 감정을 받는 대상이 돼요.

The movie was **boring**. 그 영화는 지루했다. (영화가 지루한 감정을 주는 중심)
We were **bored** by the movie. 우리는 그 영화 때문에 지루했다. (We가 지루함의 감정을 받는 대상)

interesting - interested 흥미를 일으키는 - 흥미를 느끼는	boring - bored 지루하게 하는 - 지루해 하는	exciting - excited 재미있게 하는 - 재미를 느끼는
shocking - shocked 충격적인 - 충격을 느끼는	surprising - surprised 놀라게 하는 - 놀라움을 느끼는	frightening - frightened 무섭게 하는 - 무서움을 느끼는

현재분사 / 과거분사

01 분사가 뭐예요?

분사는 형용사와 똑같이 명사를 꾸며주는 역할을 해요. 분사와 형용사의 다른 점은 형용사는 명사의 동작이나 행위를 표현해 줄 수 없으나, 분사는 명사의 [ ] 을 표현해 주는 역할을 한다는 거예요.

02 현재분사가 뭐예요?

현재분사는 동사의 원래 형태에 [ ] 를 붙여서 만들어요. 진행형을 만들 때와 똑같아요. be동사 뒤에서 또는 명사의 앞·뒤에서 명사가 직접 행위를 하게 만들어 줘요. 단, 명사를 꾸며주는 몇 개의 단어가 더 따라올 경우 현재분사는 반드시 명사 바로 [ ] 에서 꾸며줘요.

Look at the **sleeping** *tiger*! 자고 있는 호랑이를 보아라.

Do you know *the girl* **wearing** a big hat? 큰 모자를 쓰고 있는 저 소녀를 아니?

03 과거분사가 뭐예요?

과거분사는 동사의 원래 형태에 [ ] 을 붙여서 만들어요. be동사 뒤에서 또는 명사의 앞·뒤에서 명사가 행동을 당한다는 의미를 나타내요. 우리말 '~해진, 되어진'의 뜻이 돼요. 단, 명사를 꾸며주는 몇 개의 단어가 더 따라올 경우 과거분사는 명사 바로 [ ] 에서 꾸며줘요.

Used *products* can be recycled. 사용된 제품은 재활용 할 수 있다.

The car **made** in Korea is very expensive. 한국에서 만들어진 차는 매우 비싸다.

unit 02

Exercise 1

( ) 안에 알맞은 분사의 형태를 고르세요.

(1) Look at the woman (singing / sung) in the rain.

(2) It is the tallest (living / lived) tree in the world.

(2) This expensive machine isn't (working / worked) properly.

(4) (Barking / Barked) dogs seldom bite.

(4) This is one of the most (exciting / excited) games.

(6) Cars (parking / parked) on the street are very nice.

(7) He bought some books (writing / written) in English.

(8) Your room should be (cleaning / cleaned) before dinner.

(9) The concert was (interesting / interested).

(10) People buy (using / used) things at garage sales.

(11) The boy (injuring / injured) in the traffic accident was taken to the hospital.

(12) The woman (cooking / cooked) in the kitchen is my sister.

(13) I've never seen such a (boring / bored) movie.

(14) My boyfriend bought me a digital camera (making / made) in Japan.

(15) We bought some (freezing / frozen) food.

unit 02

Exercise 2

주어진 단어를 우리말에 맞게 현재분사형으로 고쳐 쓰세요.

(1) 예쁜 소녀가 나를 보고 웃고 있다.

➡ A pretty girl is ______________ at me. (smile)

(2) 끓는 물에 국수를 넣어라.

➡ Put noodles into the ______________ water. (boil)

(3) 그는 지금 공원에서 산책하고 있다.

➡ He is ______________ a walk at the park now. (take)

(4) 그는 재미있는 사람이다.

➡ He is an ______________ person. (interest)

(5) 무대 위에서 노래를 부르고 있는 소녀를 아니?

➡ Do you know the girl ______________ on the stage? (sing)

(6) 신문을 읽고 있는 분이 내 아버지시다.

➡ The man ______________ a newspaper is my father. (read)

(7) 부엌에서 요리하고 있는 소년은 누구니?

➡ Who is the boy ______________ in the kitchen? (cook)

(8) 분홍색 재킷을 입은 소녀가 내 여동생이다.

➡ The girl ______________ a pink jacket is my sister. (wear)

(9) 강아지와 함께 달리는 소년이 Kevin이야.

➡ The boy ______________ with a puppy is Kevin. (run)

(10) 나는 그녀의 웃는 얼굴을 보았다.

➡ I saw her ______________ face. (smile)

unit 02

Exercise 3

주어진 단어를 우리말에 맞게 과거분사형으로 고쳐 쓰세요.

(1) 나는 영어로 된 소설을 찾고 있다.

➡ I am looking for a novel __________ in English. (write)

(2) 이 닭고기 튀김은 매우 맛있다.

➡ This __________ chicken is very delicious. (fry)

(3) 나는 영어로 쓰여진 이메일을 받았다.

➡ I have got an e-mail __________ in English. (write)

(4) 나는 Kelly라는 여자 친구가 있다.

➡ I have a girlfriend __________ Kelly. (call)

(5) 그 소년은 자신의 도둑맞은 지갑을 찾고 있었다.

➡ The boy was looking for his __________ wallet. (steal)

(6) 그녀는 나에게 스위스에서 만들어진 시계를 사주었다.

➡ She bought me a watch __________ in Switzerland. (make)

(7) 그 냉장고 안에는 냉동식품들로 가득 차 있다.

➡ The fridge is filled with __________ foods. (freeze)

(8) 초대를 받은 많은 사람들이 오지 않았다.

➡ A lot of people __________ to the party didn't come. (invite)

(9) 너의 형이 찍은 사진은 정말 멋있다.

➡ The pictures __________ by your brother look great. (take)

(10) 나는 페인트 칠해진 의자들 몇 개를 샀다.

➡ I bought some __________ chairs. (paint)

unit 02

Jump Up!

1 빈칸에 알맞은 말을 보기 에서 골라 알맞은 형태로 고쳐 쓰세요.

보기

read a book　　break vase　　write in easy English

(1)  Look at the ______________ on the floor.

(2)  The girls ______________________ are my friends.

(3)  This book ______________________ is very popular.

vase ⓝ 꽃병, 화병
floor ⓝ 바닥
popular ⓐ 인기 있는

2 다음 빈칸에 들어갈 말로 알맞은 것을 고르세요.

(1) ______________ eat a lot of food.

① Children growing　　② Growing children
③ Children grow　　④ Grown children

(2) I like the dress ______________ in the window.

① displaying　　② display
③ displayed　　④ to display

grow ⓥ 자라다
display ⓥ 진열(전시)하다

unit 02

Writing Activity

1 보기 와 같이 두 문장을 분사를 이용하여 한 문장으로 고쳐 보세요.

보기

The lady is smiling in the classroom. ⊕ She is my English teacher.

→ The lady smiling in the classroom is my English teacher.

(1) This is a church. ⊕ It was built one hundred years ago.

→ This is a church ____________________.

(2) Look at the stars. ⊕ They are twinkling in the sky.

→ Look at the stars ____________________.

(3) The girl is my daughter. ⊕ She is crying in the park.

→ The girl ____________________.

(4) This is a digital camera. ⊕ It is made in Korea.

→ This is a digital camera ____________________.

2 각 문장을 읽고 현재분사와 과거분사를 이용해서 문장을 완성하세요.

(1) The movie disappoints you.

→ The movie is ____________.

→ You are ____________.

(2) The strange woman frightened the children.

→ The strange woman was ____________.

→ The children were ____________.

Oral Test!

1 분사란 명사의 앞·뒤에서 명사의 [ ]을 표현해주는 말이에요.

2 분사는 [ ], [ ] 이렇게 두 가지가 있어요.

3 현재분사는 동사에 [ ]를 붙여 만든 형태로 be동사 뒤 또는 명사의 앞·뒤에서 명사의 직접적인 행동을 나타내요. 명사를 꾸며주는 말이 분사 이외에도 몇 개의 단어가 더 따라 올 경우 현재분사는 반드시 명사 바로 [ ]에서 꾸며 줘요.

4 과거분사는 동사에 [ ]를 붙여 만든 형태예요. 명사가 행위의 주인이 아니라 행동을 받는, 당하는 대상일 때 과거분사를 써요.

REVIEW TARGET WORDS 주어진 단어의 철자/뜻을 쓰세요.

□ ______	ⓥ 울다	□ break	ⓥ ______
□ ______	ⓥ 놀라게 하다	□ bore	ⓥ ______
□ ______	ⓥ 충격을 주다	□ hat	ⓝ ______
□ ______	ⓥ 입다, 쓰다	□ product	ⓝ ______
□ ______	ⓥ 재생 이용하다	□ machine	ⓝ ______
□ ______	ⓐⓓ 적절히	□ bark	ⓥ ______
□ ______	ⓐⓓ 거의 … 않다	□ bite	ⓥ ______
□ ______	차고세일(중고판매)	□ injure	ⓥ ______
□ ______	교통사고	□ noodle	ⓝ ______
□ ______	ⓝ 소설	□ fry	ⓥ ______
□ ______	찾다, 구하다	□ be filled with	______
□ ______	ⓥ 얼다	□ vase	ⓝ ______
□ ______	ⓝ 바닥	□ popular	ⓐ ______
□ ______	ⓥ 진열(전시) 하다	□ twinkle	ⓥ ______
□ ______	ⓥ 실망시키다	□ dangerous	ⓐ ______

Unit 03

부사 역할의 부정사

TARGET WORDS 알고 있는 단어는 check(√) 후 뜻을 쓰고, 모르는 단어는 조사해 오세요 !

☐ bookstore	ⓝ ________	☐ airport	ⓝ ________	☐ wear	ⓥ ________
☐ turn on	________	☐ present	ⓝ ________	☐ glad	ⓐ ________
☐ full	ⓐ ________	☐ native	ⓐ ________	☐ save	ⓥ ________
☐ news	ⓝ ________	☐ bakery	ⓝ ________	☐ mail	ⓥ ________
☐ education	ⓝ ________	☐ job	ⓝ ________	☐ discussion	ⓝ ________
☐ research	ⓝ ________	☐ pocket	ⓝ ________	☐ concert	ⓝ ________
☐ school record	________	☐ bare	ⓐ ________	☐ pleased	ⓐ ________
☐ invite	ⓥ ________	☐ recycle	ⓥ ________	☐ protect	ⓥ ________
☐ environment	ⓝ ________	☐ put on	________	☐ sportswear	ⓝ ________
☐ post office	________				

Unit 03

부정사의 부사적 역할이 뭐예요?

부정사는 동사 이외에 또 다른 '동작이나 행위'를 표현해 주기 위해서 만들었어요. 동사원형 앞에 'to'를 붙여서 행동의 표현을 늘리기 위함이죠. 부정사의 부사적 용법은 크게 두 가지가 있어요. 동사의 구체적인 목적이나 이유를 나타내거나 혹은 형용사 등을 꾸며주는 역할을 해요.

동사를 꾸미는 to 부정사는 그 동사의 뜻에 더욱 구체적인 목적이나 이유를 나타낼 수 있어요. 우리말 '~하기 위하여'의 뜻이 돼요.

Sunny wanted some books, so she went to the bookstore.
Sunny는 몇 권의 책을 원했다, 그래서 서점에 갔다.

➡ She *went* to the bookstore **to buy** some books.
그녀는 몇 권의 책을 사기 위하여 서점에 갔다.

왜 Sunny는 서점에 갔을까요? 책을 사기 위해서(to buy some books) 갔다는 것을 알 수 있어요.

이처럼 to 부정사는 동사 went에 대해서 '왜' 사람이 그 행위를 했는지에 대한 목적과 이유를 설명해 주는 역할을 해요. (Why someone does something.)

'~하기 위하여'의 to 부정사를 for + 명사로 써서 목적을 나타낼 수 있어요.

She went to the bookstore **to buy** some books.
➡ She went to the bookstore **for some books**.

I went to the cafeteria **to have** lunch.
➡ I went to the cafeteria **for lunch**.

'~하기 위하여'의 뜻으로 in order to 부정사가 있는데 일상 영어에서는 in order를 거의 쓰지 않고 to 부정사만 써요.

Kelly went to the airport (**in order**) **to meet** her friend. Kelly는 친구를 만나기 위하여 공항에 갔다.
We need some money (**in order**) **to buy** food. 우리는 음식을 사기 위하여 약간의 돈이 필요하다.

부정사는 형용사 뒤에서 우리말 '~해서'(원인) 또는 '~하기에'(정도)의 뜻으로 쓰여 대개 사람의 감정에 대한 원인 혹은 태도의 원인을 나타낼 수 있어요. 보통 감정을 나타내는 형용사(happy, glad, sad, sorry, lucky, surprised, shocked, upset…etc.) 뒤에 부정사를 써요.

Nancy is *happy* **to buy** a new cellphone.
Nancy는 새 휴대폰을 사서 행복하다.

be happy 행복하다 ➡ 왜? ➡ 구입해서(to buy) 새 휴대폰을

감정을 나타내는 형용사를 제외한 나머지 일반 형용사 뒤에 오는 부정사는 우리말 '~하기에'의 뜻이 돼요.

This science book is *difficult* **to understand**. 이 과학 책은 이해하기에 어렵다.

마지막으로 too ~to와 enough to 부정사가 있는데, too를 형용사 앞에 쓰면 '필요 이상으로 지나치게'라는 부정적인 의미를 가지고 있어서 'too+형용사+to부정사'는 '너무 …해서 ~할 수 없다'는 뜻이 돼요.

Peter is **too** *small* **to wear** that shirt.
Peter는 너무 작아서 저 셔츠를 입을 수가 없다.

= Peter can't wear that shirt because he is too small.

'형용사+enough+to 부정사'는 '…할 정도로 ~하다'의 뜻이에요. 중요한 것은 enough는 형용사 뒤에 오지만 명사와 함께 쓸 때는 명사 앞에 써야 해요.

The baby is *old* **enough to walk**.
= The baby can walk because he is old enough.
그 아기는 걸을 수 있을 정도로 나이가 들었다.

She has **enough** *time* **to finish** her work.
그녀는 일을 끝낼 충분한 시간이 있다.

Unit 03

부정사의 부사적 용법

01 부정사의 부사적 용법이 뭐예요?

부정사가 부사처럼 문장에서 동사, 형용사 등을 꾸며 줄 수 있어요. 이를 to 부정사의 부사적 용법이라고 해요.

02 목적이나 의도는 어떻게 표현하나요?

to 부정사가 구체적인 '이동이나 움직임'을 나타내는 동사와 함께 쓰여 우리말 [   ]라는 뜻이 돼요. 같은 뜻으로 in order to 부정사를 쓰지만 일상영어에서는 in order를 생략하고 to 부정사만을 쓰는 것이 훨씬 더 자연스러워요.

We *went* to McDonald's **to buy** some hamburgers. 우리는 햄버거를 사기 위하여 맥도날드에 갔다.
My dad *turned* on the TV **to watch** the news. 아빠는 뉴스를 보기 위하여 TV를 켰다.

03 원인은 어떻게 표현하나요?

to 부정사는 사람의 [   ]을 표현하는 형용사 뒤에 써서 우리말 '~해서'라는 원인을 나타낼 수 있어요. 보통 흔히 쓰는 일반 형용사 뒤에 부정사를 우리는 '~하기에'로 해석해요.

I'm *pleased* **to get** a present from him. 그에게 선물을 받아서 기쁘다.
We are *glad* **to meet** you. 당신을 만나서 기쁩니다.
This cake is *easy* **to make**. 이 케이크는 만들기 쉽다.

04 too ~ to와 enough to 부정사는 뭐예요?

[too+형용사+to 부정사]는 부정의 의미가 담겨 있어서 '~하기에는 너무 …하다'로 해석해요. [형용사+enough to 부정사]는 '~할 정도로 … 하다'의 뜻이에요. enough가 형용사가 아닌 명사와 함께 쓰일 경우 enough는 명사 바로 [   ]에 써야 해요.

Kevin is **too full to eat** another pizza. Kevin은 너무 배가 불러서 더 이상 피자를 먹을 수 없다.
Your English is **good enough to talk** with a native speaker. 너의 영어는 원어민과 함께 말할 수 있을 정도로 좋다.
She has **enough money to buy** a new car. 그녀는 새 차를 살 정도로 충분한 돈을 가지고 있다.

unit 03

Exercise 1

1 ( ) 안에서 알맞은 단어를 고르세요.

(1) She saved much money (buy / to buy) an MP3 player.

(2) The students came here (to know / know) their test scores.

(3) He went to Beijing (learn / to learn) Chinese.

(4) She came here (help / to help) me.

(5) I turned on the TV (watch / to watch) the news.

(6) She has to go to the bakery (buy / to buy) some bread.

2 다음 주어진 to 부정사를 'for+명사'로 알맞게 고쳐 쓴 것을 고르세요.

(1) She went to the store to buy some fruit.

→ She went to the store (for some fruit / for buy some fruit).

(2) I went to the post office to mail a letter.

→ I went to the post office (for mail letter / for a letter).

(3) We went to Seoul to visit our friends.

→ We went to Seoul (for our friends / for to friends).

(4) Karen came to the party to meet him.

→ Karen came to the party (for him / to meet for him).

Unit 03 Exercise 2

1 주어진 빈칸에 to 또는 for를 넣어 문장을 완성하세요.

(1) I go to the library __________ read some books.

(2) We go to school __________ get an education.

(3) Korean people need English __________ get a better job.

(4) We need a listening book __________ learn listening skills.

(5) Our teacher always gives us lots of exercises __________ homework.

(6) Our teacher sometimes uses videos __________ discussion.

(7) We use the Internet __________ do research.

(8) I sometimes use my computer __________ do homework.

(9) They're going to the supermarket __________ milk and bread.

(10) We went to the restaurant __________ dinner.

2 빈칸에 too 또는 enough를 넣어 문장을 완성하세요.

(1) She is __________ young to go to school.

(2) Lisa was __________ full to eat anymore.

(3) I was hungry __________ to eat anything.

(4) My PDA is small __________ to carry in pocket.

(5) Linda is __________ young to get married.

(6) I have __________ money to buy the concert ticket.

unit 03 Exercise 3

보기 와 같이 too ~ to를 사용하여 한 문장으로 만들어 보세요.

보기

I am tired. I can't work.
→ I am too tired to work.

(1)

I am too weak. I can't carry this big schoolbag.
→ ______________________________.

(2)

My cat is too young. It can't catch a mouse.
→ ______________________________.

(3)

Tommy is too sleepy. He can't study.
→ ______________________________.

(4)

She was too sad. She couldn't talk to anyone.
→ ______________________________.

unit 03 Jump Up!

1 다음 우리말과 같도록 enough to를 이용하여 빈칸을 완성하세요.

(1) 내 학교 성적은 서울대학교에 갈 정도로 높다. (high / go)

➡ My school records are ________ ________ ________ ________ to Seoul National University.

(2) 그는 이 문제를 풀 수 있을 정도로 영리하다. (smart / solve)

➡ He is ________ ________ ________ ________ this problem.

(3) Samson은 맨손으로 호랑이를 죽일 정도로 힘이 셌다. (strong / kill)

➡ Samson was ________ ________ ________ ________ a tiger with bare hands.

school record 학교 성적
solve ⓥ 풀다, 해결하다
bare ⓐ 벌거벗은, 맨손의

2 주어진 문장을 to부정사로 고쳐 다시 쓰세요.

(1) She was surprised. ⊕ She got a letter.

➡ ____.

(2) Are you happy? ⊕ You will go to the party.

➡ ____?

(3) I was pleased. ⊕ I ate such delicious food.

➡ ____.

(4) My mom was shocked. ⊕ She heard the news.

➡ ____.

letter ⓝ 편지
be surprised 놀라다
pleased ⓐ 기뻐하는
delicious ⓐ 맛있는
news ⓝ 뉴스, 보도, 소식

unit 03

Writing Activity

그림을 보고 질문에 대한 정보를 활용하여 보기 와 같이 영작하세요.

보기

Why did Alice go to the bakery?
(buy / some bread)

She went to the bakery to buy some bread.

(1)

Why did Christina call Justin yesterday?
(invite him / to her party)

______________________________.

(2)

Why is Peter going to Pizza Hut tonight?
(have / dinner)

______________________________.

(3)

Why do they recycle old newspapers and books? (protect / the environment)

____

______________________________.

(4)

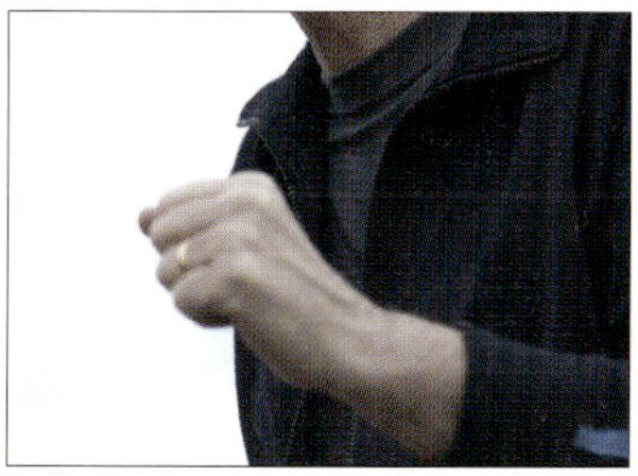

Why did Ron put on his sportswear?
(go / jogging)

______________________________.

(5)

Why did Tom go to the post office?
(mail / a letter)

______________________________.

unit 03

Oral Test!

1 부정사가 부사처럼 문장에서 동사, 형용사 등을 꾸며 주는 역할을 하는 것을 to 부정사의 [　　　] 역할(용법)이라고 해요.

2 to 부정사가 이동이나 움직임을 나타내는 동사와 함께 쓰여 그 동사의 구체적인 목적을 나타낼 때 to 부정사의 뜻은 우리말 [　　　]의 뜻이 돼요.

3 to 부정사가 사람의 감정이나 느낌을 표현하는 형용사 뒤에 위치 할 경우 우리말 '~해서'라는 [　　　]을 나타내는 역할을 해요.

4 'too+[　　　]+to 부정사', '[　　　]+enough to 부정사'의 어순으로 써요. 단 enough가 형용사가 아닌 명사와 함께 쓰일 경우에는 enough는 명사 바로 [　　　]에 써야 해요.

REVIEW TARGET WORDS

주어진 단어의 철자/뜻을 쓰세요.

☐ bookstore	ⓝ ________	☐ ________	ⓝ 공항
☐ wear	ⓥ ________	☐ ________	(전기, TV 등을) 켜다
☐ present	ⓝ ________	☐ ________	ⓐ 기쁜
☐ full	ⓐ ________	☐ ________	ⓐ (그 고장) 태생인, 원주민의
☐ save	ⓥ ________	☐ ________	ⓝ 뉴스, 소식
☐ bakery	ⓝ ________	☐ ________	ⓥ 우송하다, 우편으로 부치다
☐ education	ⓝ ________	☐ ________	ⓝ 직업
☐ discussion	ⓝ ________	☐ ________	ⓝ 연구, 조사
☐ pocket	ⓝ ________	☐ ________	ⓝ 콘서트, 음악회, 공연
☐ school record	________	☐ ________	ⓐ 벌거벗은, 맨손의
☐ pleased	ⓐ ________	☐ ________	ⓥ 초대하다
☐ recycle	ⓥ ________	☐ ________	ⓥ 막다, 보호하다
☐ environment	ⓝ ________	☐ ________	입다
☐ sportswear	ⓝ ________	☐ ________	우체국

unit 04

현재완료 계속

TARGET WORDS 알고 있는 단어는 check(√) 후 뜻을 쓰고, 모르는 단어는 조사해 오세요 !

- [ ] still (ad) ____________
- [ ] marry (v) ____________
- [ ] teach (v) ____________
- [ ] phone bill ____________
- [ ] biology (n) ____________
- [ ] collect (v) ____________
- [ ] movie star ____________
- [ ] meal (n) ____________
- [ ] company (n) ____________
- [ ] uncle (n) ____________
- [ ] freshman (n) ____________
- [ ] rise (v) ____________
- [ ] abroad (ad) ____________
- [ ] stamp (n) ____________
- [ ] begin (v) ____________
- [ ] accident (n) ____________
- [ ] elementary (a) ____________
- [ ] programmer (n) ____________
- [ ] each other ____________
- [ ] Thailand (n) ____________
- [ ] improve (v) ____________
- [ ] everywhere (ad) ____________
- [ ] history (n) ____________
- [ ] make friends ____________

Unit 04

현재완료 계속이 뭐예요?

현재완료는 '과거에 시작했는데'와 '지금은 …'을 둘 다 포함하고 있는 동사의 시제입니다. 'have + -ed(과거분사)'의 형태로 쓰며 과거분사형태가 있다고해서 과거가 아니라 '현재까지 과거분사 했(었)다'의 뜻이 되어 현재가 반드시 포함되어 있다는 것이 중요합니다.

현재완료 계속은 과거에 시작해서 현재까지 계속되고 있는 동작이나 상태를 나타내어 '쭉 ~해왔다'의 의미를 가지고 있어요.

I **started** to study two hours ago. 나는 두 시간 전에 공부를 시작했다.
I **am** still studying hard. 지금도 여전히 열심히 하고 있다.

나는 현재까지 공부했다.
→ I **have studied**.

나는 현재 두 시간 동안 공부하고 있다.
→ I **have studied for** *two hours*.

현재완료 계속은 for와 함께 쓰는데, for는 시간의 길이(a length of time)를 나타내요.

Linda and Karen **met** 10 years ago. Linda와 Karen은 10년 전에 만났다.
They **are** still friends now. 그들은 여전히 지금도 친구 사이이다.
Linda와 Karen은 10년 동안 친구로 지내왔다. (친구이다)
→ Linda and Karen **have been friends for** *10 years*.

ago는 현재완료와 함께 쓰면 안 돼요. 과거를 나타내는 표현이므로 '현재까지 …했다'의 현재완료 시제와 함께 쓸 수 없어요.

현재완료 계속은 since와 함께 쓰여요. since 뒤에 '과거연대(ex. 1999년)', 또는 '주어+과거동사'가 와서 과거에 시작된 그 특정한 시점(a period of time began)을 나타내요.

Jason **started** to work for the company in 1999.
Jason은 1999년에 그 회사에서 일을 시작했다.

He still **works** at the same company. Now it is 2009.
그는 아직도 같은 회사에서 일하고 있다. 지금은 2009년도이다.

Jason은 현재까지 일을 했다.
➡ Jason **has worked**.

Jason은 1999년부터 지금까지 그 회사에서 일하고 있다.
➡ Jason **has worked** for the company **since** 1999.

Jason은 그 회사에서 10년 동안 일하고 있다.
➡ Jason **has worked** for the company **for** 10 years.

How long~?으로 물어보는 현재완료 시제의 질문은 과거에 시작해서 지금까지의 어떤 행동이나 상태의 특정한 기간을 물어보는 것이므로 for와 since가 있는 현재완료 계속으로 대답해야 해요.

How long have you lived in London?
얼마나 오랫동안 런던에 살았나요?
➡ I **have lived** in London **for** 6 years.
6년 동안 살았어요.

How long have you known Mary?
얼마나 오랫동안 Mary를 알고 지냈나요?
➡ **I've known** her **since** 2002.
2002년부터 그녀와 알고 지냅니다.

Unit 04

현재완료 계속

01 현재완료 계속이 뭐예요?

과거에 시작한 일이나 상태가 현재에도 계속되고 있다는 뜻을 담고 있는 시제를 말해요. 과거에 일어난 사건이나 행위지만 그것이 '아직 현재와 밀접한 관련'이 있을 때 쓰는 시제가 기본적으로 완료시제예요.

02 현재완료 계속 1

현재완료 계속은 [ ] 와 함께 쓰여 시간의 길이(a length of time)를 표현해요.

Richard **has been** in Seoul **for** six months. Richard는 서울에 6개월 동안 머물러 있다.
We**'ve lived** here **for** five years. 우리는 여기서 5년 동안 살고 있다.

03 현재완료 계속 2

현재완료 계속은 [ ] 와 함께 쓰여 과거에 시작된 특정한 시점, 즉 시작점 (starting point)을 나타내요. 또한 [ ] 뒤에 주어 동사로 연결될 경우 동사는 반드시 [ ] 를 써야 해요.

Tom **has lived** in Seoul **since** 1994. Tom은 1994년 이래로 서울에 살고 있다.
I **have studied** English **since** I **was** an elementary school student. 나는 초등학교 때부터(이래로) 영어 공부를 하고 있다.

04 How long ~? 의문문

How long이 완료시제와 함께 의문문으로 쓰일 경우 그 특정한 기간을 물어보는 것이므로 [ ] 나 [ ] 를 이용해서 대답해요.

How long have they been married? 그들이 결혼한 지 얼마나 됐나요?
➡ They **have been** married **for** 20 years. 그들은 결혼한 지 20년이 되었어요.
How long have you driven a car? 얼마나 오랫동안 운전을 했나요?
➡ I **have driven** a car **since** 1998. 1998년부터 운전을 했어요.

unit 04

Exercise 1

for와 since 중 알맞은 것을 고르세요.

(1) Richard has been in Singapore (for / since) Monday.

(2) Richard has been in Singapore (for / since) four days.

(3) My uncle has lived in Seattle (for / since) 20 years.

(4) He has been a programmer (for / since) 1980.

(5) We haven't seen her (for / since) last year.

(6) My sister has worked at the hospital (for / since) 5 years.

(7) She has worked for the company (for / since) last year.

(8) I have been a teacher (for / since) 10 years.

(9) Kevin has worked for the company (for / since) 3 months.

(10) I've known his sister (for / since) September.

(11) Rachel has been in class (for / since) an hour.

(12) Jason is an English teacher. He's taught English (for / since) twenty years.

(13) Nick hasn't cleaned the house (for / since) last weekend.

(14) I haven't had a good meal (for / since) last Friday.

(15) They have studied English (for / since) ten years.

unit 04

Exercise 2

1 주어진 단어를 활용하여 현재완료 시제를 만들고 (   ) 안에 알맞은 것을 고르세요.

(1) I ____________________ (know) Rachel for (ten years / ten years ago).

(2) She ____________________ (work) here (for / since) 2004.

(3) I ____________________ (meet) her since I (am / was) a freshman in high school.

(4) Sunny ____________________ (have) a lot of problems since she (come / came) to this country.

(5) My wife and I ____________________ (know) each other since we (are / were) in elementary school.

(6) Our phone bill ____________________ (rise) since we (buy / bought) a cellphone.

2 How long을 이용한 완료 시제를 완성하세요.

(1) How long ____________________________ (you / know) Rachel?

➡ For almost twenty years.

(2) How long ____________________________ (you / study) Spanish ?

➡ Since I was an elementary school student.

(3) How long ____________________________ (your sister / work) for the hospital?

➡ Since 2005.

(4) How long ____________________________ (you / be) in Thailand?

➡ For 10 years.

Exercise 3

1 빈칸에 완료시제를 완성하고 for 또는 since를 구별해서 쓰세요.

(1) We ______________ (live) in Chicago __________ 1999.

(2) Mr. Jackson ______________ (teach) biology __________ three years.

(3) Bob ______________ (travel) abroad many times __________ he started working.

(4) Emily ______________ (improve) her Korean __________ she decided to study more.

2 보기 와 같이 현재완료 계속의 시제를 이용하여 빈칸을 완성하세요.

보기

She is a teacher.

(for six years)

She has been a teacher for six years.

(1)

Kevin's hobby is collecting stamps.

(for two years)

Kevin ______________________.

(2)

Nancy and Tom work for the company.

(since 1995)

Nancy and Tom ______________________

______________________.

(3)

It rained everywhere.

(since last night)

It ______________________

______________________.

unit 04

Jump Up!

1 다음 문장의 밑줄 친 부분 중 현재완료 계속에 해당하는 문장을 고르세요.

① I have lost my pencil.

② We've already read the book.

③ They have seen a movie star before.

④ He has slept for twenty hours.

⑤ Rachel has gone to Italy.

movie star 영화배우

2 다음 두 문장을 한 문장으로 만들기 위해 빈칸에 알맞을 말을 쓰세요.

(1) Lisa began to live in Seattle five months ago. ⊕ She still lives there.
→ Lisa ______________ in Seattle __________ five months.

(2) I first met Karen in 2006. ⊕ Karen and I are still good friends.
→ Karen and I ______________ good friends __________ 2006.

(3) Linda read two history books last Monday. ⊕ She still reads them.
→ Linda ______________ two history books __________ last Monday.

(4) Sunny lived in New York ten years ago. ⊕ She still lives there.
→ Sunny ______________ in New York __________ ten years.

(5) They got married in 2007. ⊕ They are still married.
→ They ______________ married __________ 2007.

(6) Peter started to talk on the phone 3 hours ago. ⊕ He still talks on the phone.
→ Peter ______________ on the phone __________ 3 hours.

begin ⓥ 시작하다
history ⓝ 역사
still ⓐ 여전히, 아직도
get married 결혼하다

Writing Activity

주어진 대답을 이용해 'How long+현재완료 ~?' 의문문을 만들고 주어진 단어를 활용하여 빈칸을 영작하세요.

(1)

A: ______________________________?

B: I have had my driving licence for two years.

A: ________ you ________ any accidents? (have)

B: No, I ________.

(2)

A: ______________________________?

B: I have been in Seoul since 2006.

A: ________ you ________ any friends? (make)

B: Yes, I ________ a lot of friends, but my Korean hasn't improved.

(3)

A: ______________________________?

B: I have studied English for six years, but I ________ for a long time. (not speak)

A: Neither have I. I haven't spoken English with American people, but I ________ English movies for many years. (watch)

(4)

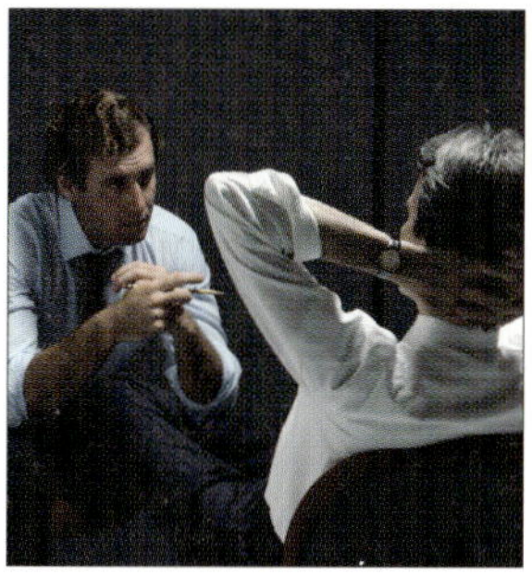

A: ______________________________?

B: I have worked here since May. But I ________ a computer programmer for 10 years. (be)

A: Have you worked for other companies?

B: Yes, I have. I ________ for three companies ________ the year 1999. (work)

unit 04

Oral Test!

1 과거부터 현재까지의 시간의 길이(a length of time)를 나타내는 현재완료 계속은 [　　　　] 와 함께 써서 구체적인 기간을 표현해 줄 수 있어요.

2 과거에 시작한 시점, 그때를 표현할 때는 [　　　　] 와 함께 써요. 또한 [　　　　] 뒤에 '주어+동사'로 연결될 경우 동사는 반드시 [　　　　] 를 써야 해요.

3 How long이 완료시제와 함께 쓰일 경우 특정한 기간을 물어보는 것이므로 [　　　　] 나 [　　　　] 를 이용해서 답해요.

REVIEW TARGET WORDS 주어진 단어의 철자/뜻을 쓰세요.

☐ ________	(ad) 여전히, 아직도	☐ company	ⓝ	________
☐ ________	ⓐ 초등학교의	☐ marry	ⓥ	________
☐ ________	ⓝ 삼촌	☐ programmer	ⓝ	________
☐ ________	ⓥ 가르치다	☐ freshman	ⓝ	________
☐ ________	서로 서로	☐ phone bill		________
☐ ________	ⓥ (값이) 오르다	☐ Thailand	ⓝ	________
☐ ________	ⓝ 생물학	☐ abroad	(ad)	________
☐ ________	ⓥ 향상시키다	☐ collect	ⓥ	________
☐ ________	ⓝ 우표	☐ everywhere	(ad)	________
☐ ________	영화배우	☐ begin	ⓥ	________
☐ ________	ⓝ 역사	☐ meal	ⓝ	________
☐ ________	ⓝ 사고	☐ make friends		________

Progress Test 1

✖ (　) 안의 동사를 이용하여 현재완료 시제 문장을 완성하세요. (1~4)

1 They ________________ in Singapore. (live)

2 I ________________ a tiger. (see)

3 Kelly ________________ her homework. (finish)

4 Peter ________________ to Egypt. I miss him. (go)

✖ 다음 문장의 (　) 안에서 알맞은 것을 고르세요. (5~7)

5 Look at the (sleeping / slept) baby.

6 English is (using / used) all over the world.

7 Justin was (watching / watched) TV last night.

✖ 다음 그림을 보고, 내용과 일치하도록 too ~ to 또는 enough to 부정사로 문장을 완성하세요. (8~9)

8 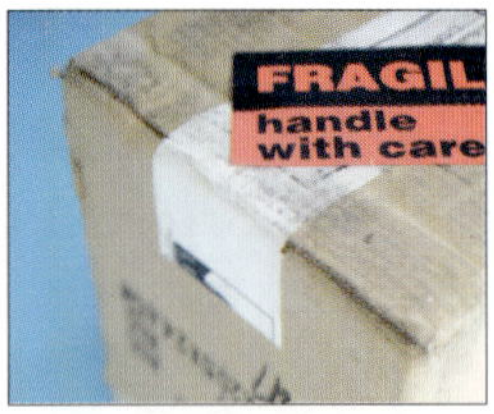

I am too weak. I can't carry this big box.

➡ ____.

9 

We are very hungry. We can eat anything.

➡ ____.

✖ 빈칸에 알맞은 것을 고르세요. (10~12)

10 Sunny has been in Singapore ________ Monday.

① since ② for

11 My dad has worked at the bank ________ 5 years.

① since ② for

12 Kelly has worked for the company ________ she finished university.

① since ② for

✖ 주어진 단어를 우리말에 맞게 현재분사형 또는 과거분사형으로 고쳐 쓰세요. (13~16)

13 나는 영어로 된 소설을 가지고 있다. (write)

➡ I have a novel ________ in English.

14 무대 위에서 춤을 추고 있는 소녀를 아니? (dance)

➡ Do you know the girl ________ on the stage?

15 그녀는 나에게 일본에서 만들어진 차를 사주었다. (make)

➡ She bought me a car ________ in Japan.

16 안경을 끼고 있는 소녀가 내 여동생이다. (wear)

➡ The girl ________ glasses is my sister.

✖ 주어진 대답을 이용해 How long + 현재완료 ~? 의문문을 만들어 보세요. (17~18)

17

____

______________________________?

I have worked for the company since 2002.

18

____

______________________________?

I have studied English for five years.

✖ 다음 두 문장을 한 문장으로 만들어 보세요. (19~20)

19 We started to live in Seattle in 2005. We still live here.

➡ ______________________________.

20 Lisa began to teach English five months ago. She still teaches English.

➡ ______________________________.

unit 05

2, 4, 5형식 동사

TARGET WORDS 알고 있는 단어는 check(√) 후 뜻을 쓰고, 모르는 단어는 조사해 오세요 !

☐ look	ⓥ ______		☐ seem	ⓥ ______		☐ feel	ⓥ ______
☐ taste	ⓥ ______		☐ sound	ⓥ ______		☐ take a picture	______
☐ terrible	ⓐ ______		☐ allow	ⓥ ______		☐ serious	ⓐ ______
☐ rough	ⓐ ______		☐ voice	ⓝ ______		☐ upset	ⓐ ______
☐ green tea	______		☐ send	ⓥ ______		☐ message	ⓝ ______
☐ stand up	______		☐ dead	ⓐ ______		☐ advise	ⓥ ______
☐ mental hospital	______		☐ cheer up	______		☐ thirsty	ⓐ ______
☐ partner	ⓝ ______						

Unit 05

2, 4, 5형식이 뭐예요?

주어의 성질이나 상태를 나타낼 때 be동사 뒤에 형용사를 써서 표현하는 것을 앞서 배웠어요. be동사와 같은 역할로 look(~처럼 보이다), sound(~처럼 들리다), smell(~처럼 냄새가 나다)과 같은 감각동사는 주어의 상태나 성질을 좀 더 구체적으로 설명해 주기 위해서 쓰는 2형식 동사예요. 감각동사 뒤에는 반드시 '형용사'를 써야 하고, '명사'를 쓰려면 전치사 like의 도움을 받아 '감각동사+like+명사'로 써야 해요.

She **looks** *angry*.
그녀는 화난 것처럼 보인다.

They **seem** *happy*.
그들은 행복한 것처럼 보인다.

'feel+형용사(~하게 느끼다)', 'taste+형용사(~한 맛이 나다)'의 감각동사도 있어요.

I **feel** *thirsty*. 갈증이 나요.　　This cake **tastes** *delicious*. 이 케이크는 맛있다.

4형식 동사는 상대방에게 '~을 주다'란 뜻을 가진 동사들을 말해요. 우리말 '~에게 선물을 주다'라고 하면 동사 give 뒤에 선물을 받는 사람명사를 쓰고 바로 뒤에 선물(gift)이라는 사물명사를 써야 하기 때문에 목적어가 2개 있어야 해요.

Maria **gave** *her father* a cake. (4형식)
Maria는 그녀의 아빠에게 케이크를 드렸다.

I **gave** a gift (**to** *my girlfriend*). (3형식)
나는 내 여자 친구에게 선물을 주었다.

4형식 동사 뒤에 바로 선물을 받는 사람이 아닌 선물이라는 대상을 먼저 쓸 때는 사람명사 앞에 반드시 전치사를 써야 해요.

- to를 쓰는 동사: give, send, show, tell, teach, write, pass, lend, etc.
- for를 쓰는 동사: make, buy, get, cook, sing, etc.

Mom **made** *me* some cookies. (4형식 문장)
엄마는 나에게 과자를 좀 만들어 주셨다.
= Mom **made** some cookies **for** *me*. (3형식 문장)

5형식 동사는 주어, 동사, 목적어만으로는 문장의 의미가 완전히 전달되지 못해서 목적어에 대한 보충 설명(목적격 보어)을 해주는 말을 하나 더 써주어야 비로소 완전한 문장이 되는 동사를 말해요.

• 목적격 보어로 명사를 쓰는 경우: 목적어의 동일한 대상, 이름을 말해줘요.

He is a doctor. (2형식)
그는 의사이다.
= We **think** him *a doctor*. (5형식)
우리는 그가 의사라고 생각한다.

• 목적격 보어로 형용사를 쓰는 경우: 목적어의 성질이나 상태를 말해줘요.

She is beautiful. (2형식)
그녀는 아름답다
= Everyone **believes** her *beautiful*. (5형식)
모든 사람은 그녀가 아름답다고 믿는다.

• 목적격 보어로 to 부정사를 쓰는 경우: 목적어의 동작이나 행동하는 것을 말해줘요.

He **asked** me *to take* pictures. (5형식)
그는 나에게 사진을 찍어달라고 요청했다.

Mom **told** me *to wash* my hands. (5형식)
엄마는 나에게 손을 씻으라고 말했다.

Unit 05

2, 4, 5형식 동사

01 감각동사가 뭐예요?

주어의 상태나 성질을 표현해 줄 때 보어로 [ ] 를 사용해요. be동사 보다 좀 더 구체적인 주어의 상태나 성질을 표현해주는 감각동사는 뒤에 반드시 [ ] 를 쓰고 부사를 쓰면 안 돼요.

She **looks** *happy*. 그녀는 행복한 것처럼 보인다.
His story **sounds** *strange*. 그의 이야기는 이상한 것처럼 들린다.
His feet **smell** *terrible*. 그의 발에서는 지독한 냄새가 난다.

02 4형식 동사가 뭐예요?

상대방에게 '~을 해주다', '~을 만들어주다', '~을 보여 주다'의 뜻을 가진 동사들을 4형식 동사라고 해요. 그 의미의 특성상 사람명사와 사물명사, 이렇게 목적어가 2개 있어야 해요. 단, 동사 뒤에 사물명사가 사람명사보다 먼저 나오면 반드시 [ ] 를 써야 해요.

- [ ] 를 쓰는 동사 : give, send, show, tell, teach, write, pass, lend, etc.
- [ ] 를 쓰는 동사 : make, buy, get, cook, sing, etc.

Kevin **wrote** *me* a letter.
→ Kevin **wrote** a letter **to** *me*.
Kevin은 나에게 편지를 썼다.

He **bought** *his son* a toy.
→ He **bought** a toy **for** *his son*.
그는 그의 아들에게 장난감을 사 주었다.

03 5형식 동사가 뭐예요?

주어, 동사, 목적어만으로 문장의 의미가 완전히 전달되지 못해서 목적어에 대한 보충 설명을 하나 더 써주어야 의미가 전달되는 동사를 말해요. 목적격 보어로서 [ ] 는 목적어의 동일한 대상, [ ] 는 목적어의 성질이나 상태, [ ] 는 목적어가 '~하는 것' 이라는 뜻의 동작이나 행동을 나타내요.

His mother **made** him *a doctor*. 그의 엄마는 그를 의사로 만들었다.
We **think** Linda *smart*. 우리는 Linda가 영리하다고 생각한다.
My dad **allowed** me *to go* to the party. 아빠는 내가 파티에 가는 것을 허락하셨다.

unit 05

Exercise 1

1 (　　) 안에서 알맞은 단어를 고르세요.

(1) The room smelled very (terrible / terribly).

(2) They seem (happy / happily).

(3) That food smells (bad / badly).

(4) He looks (wise / wisely).

(5) Seo-yoon (look / looks) (strongly / strong).

(6) The cookies in the box (tastes / taste) (sweetly / sweet).

(7) You look (serious / seriously).

(8) This paper (feels / feel) (rough / roughly).

2 우리말과 같은 뜻이 되도록 알맞은 감각동사를 보기 에서 골라 써 넣으세요. (복수, 과거형 유의)

보기

taste　　look　　smell　　sound　　feel

(1) 그녀의 목소리는 아름답게 들린다.

→ Her voice ______________ beautiful.

(2) 그 피자는 맛있는 냄새가 난다.

→ The pizza ______________ good.

(3) 그들은 기분이 별로 좋지 않다.

→ They don't ______________ good.

(4) 담임 선생님은 정말 화가 나 보였다.

→ Our homeroom teacher ______________ really upset.

(5) 이 녹차는 좋은 맛이 난다.

→ This green tea ______________ nice.

unit 05 Exercise 2

1 (   ) 안에서 알맞은 것을 고르세요.

(1) Jason teaches (us English / English us).

(2) I showed (my picture her / her my picture).

(3) She sent (me an e-mail / an e-mail me).

(4) Mom made (us some cookies / some cookies us).

(5) She gave (him chocolates / chocolates him) on Valentine's Day.

(6) I will buy (my son a bike / a bike my son).

(7) I want to buy (for you a gift / you a gift).

(8) This is Karen's hat. Can you give (it to her / her it)?

2 전치사 to와 for 중에서 알맞은 것을 고르세요.

(1) My mom bought a new cellphone (to / for) me.

(2) She wrote an e-mail (to / for) her friend.

(3) My brother gave your message (to / for) me.

(4) She lends some money (to / for) me.

(5) My grandfather told many interesting stories (to / for) me.

(6) He made a nice chair (to / for) his daughter.

unit 05 # Exercise 3

1 ( ) 안에서 알맞은 것을 고르세요.

(1) He asked her (to stand / stand) up.

(2) Nancy asked his children (be / to be) quiet.

(3) We found our dog (dead / to dead).

(4) The doctor advised the man (to go / go) to a mental hospital.

(5) The movie made him (a big star / to a big star).

(6) Mom didn't allow me (to spend / spend) a lot of money.

(7) Please call (I / me) Ron.

(8) He found the test (difficult / difficulty).

2 ( ) 안의 동사를 알맞은 형태로 바꿔 써 보세요.

(1) They asked me ____________ (take) pictures.

(2) She asked me ____________ (help) her.

(3) I want you ____________ (come) on time.

(4) He asked her ____________ (marry) him.

(5) She told me ____________ (cheer) up.

(6) My dad allowed me ____________ (go) to the party.

(7) My doctor advised me ____________ (exercise) every day.

Jump Up!

1 다음 그림에 맞게 4형식 문장과 3형식 문장을 쓰세요.

(1) 

(some flowers / Karen)

Tom gave ______________________________.

Tom gave ______________________________.

(2) 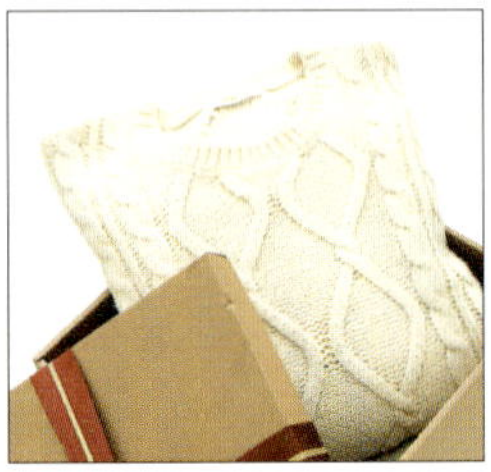

(a sweater / me)

My friend made _________________________.

My friend made _________________________.

sweater ⓝ 스웨터 (두꺼운 털 셔츠)

2 다음 그림에 맞는 형용사를 보기 에서 골라 동사 look을 이용하여 문장을 완성하세요.

(1)  (2)  (3)  (4) 

보기

angry thirsty happy hungry

thirsty ⓐ 목마른

(1) She _________________________. (2) She _________________________.

(3) They ________________________. (4) They ________________________.

unit 05

Writing Activity

| 보기 와 같이 주어진 표현을 이용하여 5형식 문장으로 완성하세요.

(1) 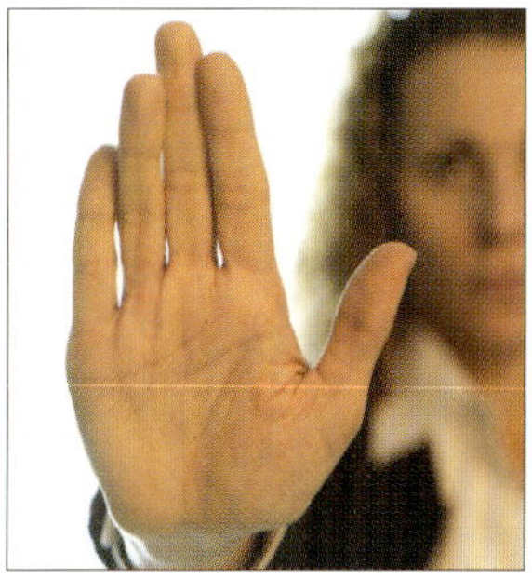

The woman said to me, "You should stop here."

➡ The woman ______________________________.

(tell)

(2) 

The doctor said, "Peter, you should lose ten kilograms."

➡ The doctor ______________________________.

(advise)

(3) 

"Please help me with this question," Lisa said to her partner.

➡ Lisa ______________________________ her with that question. (ask)

(4) 

"Would you like to have a cup of coffee with me after class?" Sunny said to Nancy.

➡ Sunny ______________________________ with her after class. (ask)

unit 05 Oral Test!

1 감각동사 뒤에는 반드시 [   ] 를 쓰고 부사를 쓰지 않아요.

2 4형식 문장을 3형식 문장으로 만들 때 반드시 [   ] 가 필요해요.

- [   ] 를 쓰는 동사: give, send, show, tell, teach, write, pass, lend, etc.
- [   ] 를 쓰는 동사: make, buy, get, cook, sing, etc.

3 목적격 보어로서 [   ] 는 목적어의 동일한 대상, [   ] 는 목적어의 성질이나 상태, [   ] 는 목적어가 '~하는 것' 이라는 뜻의 동작이나 행동을 나타내요.

REVIEW TARGET WORDS 주어진 단어의 철자/뜻을 쓰세요.

□ look	ⓥ ______	□ ______	ⓥ ~처럼 보이다
□ feel	ⓥ ______	□ ______	ⓥ ~처럼 맛이 나다
□ sound	ⓥ ______	□ ______	사진을 찍다
□ terrible	ⓐ ______	□ ______	ⓥ 허락하다
□ serious	ⓐ ______	□ ______	ⓐ 거칠거칠한
□ voice	ⓝ ______	□ ______	ⓐ 기분이 상한, 화가 난
□ green tea	______	□ ______	ⓥ 보내다, 부치다
□ message	ⓝ ______	□ ______	일어서다
□ dead	ⓐ ______	□ ______	ⓥ 충고하다
□ mental hospital	______	□ ______	힘내다
□ thirsty	ⓐ ______	□ ______	ⓝ 동료, 상대방

unit 06

동명사

TARGET WORDS 알고 있는 단어는 check(√) 후 뜻을 쓰고, 모르는 단어는 조사해 오세요 !

단어	품사	뜻	단어	품사	뜻	단어	품사	뜻
☐ necessary	ⓐ	________	☐ climb	ⓥ	________	☐ rock	ⓝ	________
☐ health	ⓝ	________	☐ ski	ⓥ	________	☐ regret	ⓥ	________
☐ school days		________	☐ rest	ⓝ	________	☐ sell	ⓥ	________
☐ be proud of		________	☐ foreign	ⓐ	________	☐ language	ⓝ	________
☐ midnight	ⓝ	________	☐ dark	ⓐ	________	☐ insist	ⓥ	________
☐ be interested in		________	☐ stand	ⓥ	________	☐ neighbor	ⓝ	________
☐ be afraid of		________	☐ kite	ⓝ	________	☐ continue	ⓥ	________
☐ on one's way home		________	☐ prepare	ⓥ	________	☐ beach	ⓝ	________
☐ over and over again		________	☐ quit	ⓥ	________	☐ course	ⓝ	________
☐ especially	ⓐⓓ	________	☐ work out		________	☐ tidy	ⓥ	________

Unit 06

동명사가 뭐예요?

동명사는 부정사와 마찬가지로 동사 외에 또 다른 동작이나 행동을 설명해 줄 수 있는 역할이에요. '동사원형 + -ing' 로 만들어 부정사와는 달리 문장 속에서 명사처럼만 쓰이는 것으로 동작의 의미를 가진 명사라고 생각하면 돼요.

주어자리에서 주어의 '행위나 동작'이 필요할 경우에 써요. 우리말 '~하는 것은', '~하기는'의 뜻이에요.

Learning English is very important.
영어를 배우는 것은 매우 중요하다.
(동명사 주어(Learning English)는 주어의 동작, 행동 표현 가능)

Studying English is necessary.
영어를 공부하는 것은 필수다.

동사 뒤에 목적어 자리에서 목적어의 '행위나 동작'이 필요할 경우에 써요. 우리말 '하는 것을'의 뜻이에요.

Nancy *loves* **climbing** rocks.
Nancy는 암벽 타는 것을 좋아한다.

명사나 형용사가 보어로 쓰이지만 동작이나 행동의 내용이 보어일 때는 동명사를 써요. 우리말 '~하는 것이다'의 뜻이에요.

My hobby *is* **jogging** (=**to jog**).
내 취미는 조깅하는 것이다.

주어와 보어로 쓰인 동명사와 부정사는 큰 차이가 없어서 서로 바꿔 써도 돼요.

전치사 뒤에는 주로 명사가 와야 되지만 '동작이나 행동'이 필요할 때는 동명사를 써야 해요. 우리말 '~하는 것', '~것'의 뜻이 돼요.

I'm fond *of* **listening** to music.
나는 음악 듣는 것을 좋아한다.

Bob is good *at* **skiing**.
Bob은 스키 타는 것을 잘한다. (스키를 잘 탄다.)

동명사만을 목적어로 가지길 좋아하는 동사가 따로 있어요.

enjoy (~하는 것을 즐기다) finish (~하는 것을 끝내다) give up (~하기를 포기하다)
avoid (~하는 것을 피하다) mind (~하는 것을 꺼리다) stop (~하기를 멈추다)

위의 동사들은 대표적으로 목적어로 동명사만을 사용해요.

Maria *gave up* **smoking**.
Maria는 담배를 끊었다.

동명사의 부정은 동명사 앞에 not을 써요.

You will regret **not taking** the job.
당신은 그 직업을 갖지 않은 것을 후회하게 될 것입니다.

Unit 06

동명사

01 동명사가 뭐예요?

동명사란 '동사원형 + −ing' 의 형태로 문장 속에서 동작이나 행위를 표현할 수 있어서 동작의 의미를 가진 ______ 라고 생각하면 돼요.

02 동명사는 문장에서 어떤 역할을 하나요?

1 ______ 역할: 문장의 주어 자리에 '동작이나 행동'을 표현할 때 써요.

Dancing salsa was interesting. 살사 춤을 추는 것은 재미있었다.

2 ______ 역할: 동사 뒤에서 즉, 목적어 자리에서 '동작이나 행동'을 표현할 때 써요.

I finished **cleaning** my room a few hours ago. 난 몇 시간 전에 내 방 청소를 끝냈다.

3 ______ 역할: be동사 뒤의 보어 자리에서 '동작이나 행동'을 표현할 때 써요.

Her hobby is **taking** pictures of ghosts. 그녀의 취미는 귀신 사진을 찍는 것이다.

4 전치사+ ______ 의 역할: 전치사 뒤에는 언제나 명사를 쓰지만 '동작이나 행위'를 표현하려면 동명사를 써야 해요.

I thought of **buying** a house. 나는 집 사는 것을 생각했었다.

03 동명사만을 목적어로 가지는 동사가 따로 있나요?

enjoy (~하는 것을 즐기다)
finish (~하는 것을 끝내다)
give up (~하기를 포기하다)
avoid (~하는 것을 피하다)
mind (~하는 것을 꺼리다)
stop (~하는 것을 멈추다)

위의 동사들은 대표적으로 목적어로 동명사만을 사용해요.

04 동명사의 부정은 어떻게 만들어요?

동명사의 부정은 동명사 앞에 ______ 을 써주면 돼요.

She regrets **not studying** English during school days. 그녀는 학창 시절에 영어 공부를 하지 않은 것을 후회한다.

Unit 06

Exercise 1

1 보기 와 같이 밑줄 친 부분이 문장에서 하는 역할을 고르세요.

보기

His job is **teaching** English at school. 보어

(1) **Taking** a good rest is the most important thing. ________

(2) She likes **jogging** at night. ________

(3) Karl enjoys **playing** basketball. ________

(4) Her job is **selling** many kinds of flowers. ________

(5) My dream is **making** a lot of money. ________

(6) Would you mind **opening** the window? ________

(7) **Reading** in a dark room is not good for the eyes. ________

(8) My hobby is **watching** movies. ________

(9) **Learning** foreign languages is interesting. ________

(10) Karen finished **studying** at midnight. ________

2 주어진 단어를 알맞은 동명사로 고쳐서 빈칸에 써 넣으세요.

(1) He is proud of ________ (be) a teacher.

(2) Kelly insisted on ________ (come) with us.

(3) We're excited about ________ (go) to Thailand.

(4) Thank you for ________ (open) the door.

(5) Are you interested in ________ (watch) the movie with us?

(6) Are you afraid of ________ (fly) in small planes?

Unit 06

Exercise 2

1 같은 뜻을 가진 문장이 되도록 밑줄 친 부분을 동명사로 고쳐서 다시 쓰세요.

(1) The boy began to sing.

→ ______________________________.

(2) Ted hates to do his homework.

→ ______________________________.

(3) She can't stand to wait in a long line.

→ ______________________________.

(4) Mary likes to sit in front of the television.

→ ______________________________.

(5) They started to fight.

→ ______________________________.

(6) Does she love to fly kites?

→ ______________________________?

(7) His neighbor continued to talk about Sunny's car.

→ ______________________________.

2 밑줄 친 부분에 유의하여 다음을 우리말로 해석하세요

(1) Why do you dislike living in Seoul?

→ ______________________________?

(2) My mom's hobby is swimming.

→ ______________________________.

Unit 06 Exercise 3

1 ( ) 안에서 알맞은 단어를 고르세요.

(1) We enjoy (to listen / listening) to the songs.

(2) It stopped (to rain / raining) a few minutes ago.

(3) David quit (to smoke / smoking).

(4) Would you mind (to close / closing) the door?

(5) I can't avoid (to answer / answering) the question.

(6) I couldn't enjoy (to watch / watching) the movie.

2 그림에 맞는 표현을 주어진 단어를 활용하여 완성하세요.

(1) 

Ron ______________ at the clock. (look, kept)

(2) 

Would you ______________ the window? (close, mind)

(3) 

They ______________ in the mountains. (ski, enjoy)

Unit 06

Jump Up!

동명사와 부정사의 표현 중 빈칸에 알맞은 것을 고르세요.

(1) I enjoyed _________ with my family at the beach last summer.

① being　　② to be

(2) I've decided _________ for another job.

① looking　　② to look

(3) Justin, would you mind _________ this letter on your way home?

① mailing　　② to mail

(4) At last, I finished _________ for the final exam.

① preparing　　② to prepare

(5) Do you expect _________ this course? If so, you'd better work harder.

① passing　　② to pass

(6) Let's get together tonight. I want to talk about _________ a new business.

① opening　　② to open

(7) Why do you keep _________ me the same question over and over again?

① asking　　② to ask

(8) Thanks for _________ to me and for _________ me the books. I really enjoyed _________ them, especially *The Harry Potter* series.

① to write – sending – to read

② writing – sending – reading

beach ⓝ 해변, 바닷가
job ⓝ 직업
on one's way home 집에 가는 도중에
prepare ⓥ 준비하다
expect ⓥ 예상(생각)하다
course ⓝ 과목, 강좌
business ⓝ 장사, 사업,
over and over again 되풀이해서, 몇 번이고
especially ⓐⓓ 특히

Writing Activity

다음 표는 Nancy에 관한 정보입니다. 동명사를 이용하여 표의 내용과 일치하도록 영작하세요.

	avoid	don't mind	be interested in	hate	enjoy	can't stand
take pictures					√	
get a job at a hotel			√			
wake up early						√
wash her feet				√		
work out at night	√					
tidy her room		√				

보기

Nancy avoids working out at night.

(1) Nancy ______________________________.

(2) Nancy ______________________________.

(3) Nancy ______________________________.

(4) Nancy ______________________________.

(5) Nancy ______________________________.

Unit 06

Oral Test!

1 동명사란 '동사원형 + -ing'의 형태로 문장에서 동작의 표현을 가지는 [ ] 라고 생각하면 돼요.

2 [ ] 역할: 문장의 주어 자리에서 '동작이나 행동'을 표현할 때 써요.

3 [ ] 역할: 동사 뒤에서 즉, 목적어 자리에서 '동작이나 행동'을 표현할 때 써요.

4 [ ] 역할: be동사 뒤의 보어 자리에서 '동작이나 행동'을 표현할 때 써요.

5 전치사+ [ ] 의 역할 : 전치사 뒤는 언제나 명사를 쓰지만 '동작이나 행위'를 표현하려면 동명사를 써야 해요.

6 enjoy (~하는 것을 즐기다) finish (~하는 것을 끝내다) give up (~하기를 포기하다)
avoid (~하는 것을 피하다) mind (~하는 것을 꺼리다) stop (~하는 것을 멈추다)

위의 동사들은 대표적으로 목적어로 [ ] 만을 사용해요.

7 동명사의 부정은 동명사 앞에 [ ] 을 써주면 돼요.

REVIEW TARGET WORDS 주어진 단어의 철자/뜻을 쓰세요.

☐ necessary	ⓐ ______	☐ ______	ⓥ (~을) 기어오르다
☐ rock	ⓝ ______	☐ ______	ⓝ 건강
☐ ski	ⓥ ______	☐ ______	ⓥ 후회하다
☐ school days	______	☐ ______	ⓝ 휴식
☐ sell	ⓥ ______	☐ ______	ⓐ 어두운
☐ foreign	ⓐ ______	☐ ______	ⓝ 언어
☐ midnight	ⓝ ______	☐ ______	~을 자랑스러워하다
☐ insist	ⓥ ______	☐ ______	~에 관심(흥미)이 있다
☐ be afraid of	______	☐ ______	ⓥ 참다, 견디다
☐ kite	ⓝ ______	☐ ______	ⓝ 이웃 (사람)
☐ continue	ⓥ ______	☐ ______	ⓥ ~을 그만두다
☐ beach	ⓝ ______	☐ ______	집에 가는 도중에
☐ prepare	ⓥ ______	☐ ______	ⓝ 과목, 강좌
☐ over and over again	______	☐ ______	ⓐⓓ 특히
☐ work out	______	☐ ______	ⓥ 정돈하다

unit 07
수동태

TARGET WORDS 알고 있는 단어는 check(√) 후 뜻을 쓰고, 모르는 단어는 조사해 오세요 !

☐ paint	ⓥ	______	☐ picture	ⓝ	______	☐ mirror	ⓝ	______
☐ invite	ⓥ	______	☐ temple	ⓝ	______	☐ destroy	ⓥ	______
☐ rice	ⓝ	______	☐ grow	ⓥ	______	☐ hire	ⓥ	______
☐ film	ⓝ	______	☐ careless	ⓐ	______	☐ accident	ⓝ	______
☐ package	ⓝ	______	☐ neighbor	ⓝ	______	☐ wallet	ⓝ	______
☐ fix	ⓥ	______	☐ deliver	ⓥ	______	☐ light bulb		______
☐ invent	ⓥ	______	☐ government	ⓝ	______	☐ tax	ⓝ	______
☐ drink	ⓝ	______	☐ drug	ⓝ	______	☐ ingredient	ⓝ	______
☐ serve	ⓥ	______	☐ open	ⓥ	______			

unit 07

수동태가 뭐예요?

우리가 흔히 만나는 거의 모든 문장은 주어가 동사의 주인이 되어 그 행위나 행동을 직접 하는 것이 대부분이에요. 우리는 그것을 '능동태(active voice)'라고 하고 주어가 동작을 하는 주인이 아닌 '동작을 받는(당하는) 대상'의 의미를 나타내는 형태를 '수동태(passive voice)'라고 해요.

Lisa **painted** the picture. Lisa가 그 그림을 그렸다. (능동태)

The picture **was painted** by Lisa. 그 그림은 Lisa에 의해 그려졌다. (수동태)

수동태는 그 행위를 받는(당한) 대상을 중요하게 나타내고 싶거나 또는 강조하고 싶기 때문에 문장 맨 앞인 주어 자리로 보내는 거예요. 따라서 목적어를 강조하기 위한 것이고, 당연히 문장에서 목적어가 없다면 수동태로 고칠 수가 없어요. 왜냐하면 강조할 대상이 없기 때문이죠.

수동태의 동사 형태는 'be동사+과거분사'로 쓰고 원래 주인이었던 주어는 'by+목적격'으로 만들어 문장 뒤로 보내요. 우리가 앞서 배운 '과거분사+명사'에서도 명사가 행동의 주인이 아닌 '행동을 받은(당한)' 대상이 된다는 것을 배웠어요. 수동태도 행동을 당하는 대상을 주어에 두고 주어에 맞는 'be동사+과거분사'를 사용해서 문장을 만드는 거예요.

a broken mirror 깨진(부서진) 거울

➡ A mirror **was broken** by Nancy. 거울이 Nancy에 의해서 깨졌다.

a made rug 만들어진 깔개

➡ A rug **is made** by my aunt. 깔개가 내 고모에 의해서 만들어졌다.

수동태의 부정문은 be동사가 있을 때는 언제나 be동사 뒤에 not을 써요. 수동태를 의문문으로 만들 때도 be동사를 문장 맨 앞으로 보내고, Yes/No를 이용해 be동사로 대답해요.

I am not invited to the party.
나는 파티에 초대받지 못했다.

Is this book **written** by him?
이 책이 그에 의해서 쓰여진 것인가요?
→ Yes, it **is**. 네. / No, it **isn't**. 아니오.

행위자를 표시해 주는 '전치사 by+명사'는 그 행위를 누가 했는지가 중요할 때 써요.

The magazine is read **by a lot of people**. 그 잡지는 많은 사람들에 의해 읽혀진다.

The telephone was invented **by Graham Bell**. 전화는 Graham Bell에 의해 발명되었다.

행위자의 주체가 일반 사람이거나(by people), 언급하지 않아도 누구나 알 수 있는 경우, 마지막으로 누구에 의해서 행해졌는지 알 수 없거나 중요하지 않은 경우에는 'by+명사(목적격)'을 쓰지 않아요.

The temple **was destroyed** in 1900. 그 사원은 1900년에 파괴되었다. (누가 파괴했는지 모름)

English **is spoken** all over the world. 영어는 전 세계에서 쓰인다. (일반 사람들)

Rice **is grown** in Korea. 쌀은 한국에서 재배된다. (누가 재배하는지는 중요하지 않음)

Alice **was hired** as a programmer. Alice는 프로그래머로 채용되었다. (누구나 사장이 채용했다는 것을 알 수 있음.)

Unit 07 수동태

01 수동태가 뭐예요?

주어가 직접 동사를 다루어 행위를 하는 경우를 '능동태(active voice)'라고 하고, 주어가 행위나 동작을 당하는(받는) 대상일 경우에는 주어 자리에 대상에 해당하는 명사를 쓰고 동사를 '______ + ______' 형태로 만든 문장을 '수동태(passive voice)'라고 해요.

02 수동태는 왜 쓰는 건가요?

영어는 중요한 말을 문장 맨 앞으로 보내 그 말을 주어로 씀으로써 강조하거나 중요성을 표현해요. 또 행위자에는 관심이 없고 행위를 받는 대상을 중심으로 표현하는 문장이에요.

My mom **loves** me. 엄마는 나를 사랑한다.

→ I **am loved** by my mom. 나는 엄마에게 사랑을 받는다.

Spielberg **made** that film. Spielberg가 저 영화를 만들었다.

→ That film **was made** by Spielberg. 저 영화는 Spielberg에 의해서 만들어 졌다.

03 부정문과 의문문은 어떻게 만드나요?

수동태 또한 be동사가 들어가 있는 문장이므로 앞서 배운 것처럼 언제나 be동사 뒤에 ______을 붙여서 부정문을 만들어요. 수동태의 의문문은 ______ 동사를 문장 맨 앞으로 보내서 만들어요.

The food **wasn't cooked** by her. 그 요리는 그녀에 의해 요리된 것이 아니다.
Was the window **broken** by them? 그 창문은 그들에 의해 깨졌니?
→ Yes, it **was**. / No, it **wasn't**.

unit 07

Exercise 1

다음 주어진 동사의 과거형과 'be+과거분사형'을 써 보세요.

동사원형	과거	be+과거분사
(1) break	________	be ________
(2) ask	________	be ________
(3) buy	________	be ________
(4) do	________	be ________
(5) know	________	be ________
(6) take	________	be ________
(7) write	________	be ________
(8) make	________	be ________
(9) build	________	be ________
(10) speak	________	be ________
(11) steal	________	be ________
(12) tell	________	be ________
(13) draw	________	be ________
(14) paint	________	be ________
(15) lose	________	be ________
(16) teach	________	be ________
(17) give	________	be ________
(18) grow	________	be ________

unit 07 **Exercise 2**

1 (　) 안에서 알맞은 단어를 고르세요.

(1) This window (broke / was broken) by children.

(2) The teacher (loves / is loved) us.

(3) The newspaper (reads / is read) by many people.

(4) They (invited / were invited) to the party by her.

(5) Careless driving (causes / is caused) many accidents.

(6) The teacher (helps / is helped) us.

(7) We (helped / are helped) by the teacher.

2 주어진 문장을 수동태의 부정문으로 다시 쓰세요.

(1) The letter was written by Justin.

➡ ______________________________.

(2) This house was built 100 years ago.

➡ ______________________________.

(3) The package was mailed by Peter.

➡ ______________________________.

(4) Susan was hired by that company.

➡ ______________________________.

(5) The children were found by a neighbor last night.

➡ ______________________________.

unit 07 Exercise 3

1 주어진 문장을 수동태로 고쳐서 다시 써 보세요.

(1) Books change your life.

➡ ______________________________.

(2) Karen finished the work.

➡ ______________________________.

(3) Lucy broke the glasses.

➡ ______________________________.

(4) Many people saw the accident.

➡ ______________________________.

(5) Christina took these pictures.

➡ ______________________________.

2 주어진 문장을 수동태 의문문으로 고쳐 쓰고 그 대답을 완성하세요.

(1) She wrote this e-mail.

➡ ______________________? Yes, ____________.

(2) He did the work.

➡ ______________________? No, ____________.

(3) My wallet was stolen on the subway.

➡ ______________________? Yes, ____________.

(4) My dad fixed these bikes.

➡ ______________________? No, ____________.

unit 07

Jump Up!

1 주어진 단어를 활용하여 수동태 문장을 완성하세요.

(1) 

(deliver / our mail)

______________________ by Mr. Kevin.

(2) 

(eat / the cake / yesterday)

__________________________ by them.

deliver ⓥ 배달하다

2 다음 주어진 단어를 활용하여 능동태, 수동태 문장을 완성해 보세요.

(1) Thomas Edison / the light bulb / invent

➡ Thomas Edison ____________________________________.

➡ The light bulb ____________________________________.

(2) The government / taxes / collect

➡ The government ____________________________________.

➡ Taxes ____________________________________.

(3) Leo Tolstoy / the book *War and Peace* / write

➡ Leo Tolstoy ____________________________________.

➡ The book *War and Peace* ____________________________.

light bulb 백열전구
invent ⓥ 발명하다
government ⓝ 정부
collect
ⓥ (세금 등을) 징수하다
tax ⓝ 세금

unit 07

Writing Activity

주어진 문장을 수동태로 바꾸고, 'by+명사'가 불필요할 때는 생략해서 영작하세요.

(1) People drink Coca-Cola all over the world.

➡ ______________________________.

(2) John Pemberton invented the drink in 1886.

➡ ______________________________.

(3) He sold it as a drug.

➡ ______________________________.

(4) People do not know the ingredients of Coca-Cola.

➡ ______________________________.

(5) The McDonald brothers opened the first Mcdonald's restaurant in California in 1949.

➡ ______________________________

______________________________.

(6) The restaurant served only three things: hamburgers, French fries, and milkshakes.

➡ ______________________________

______________________________.

(7) People eat more than 40 million hamburgers every day.

➡ ______________________________.

unit 07

Oral Test!

1 행위나 동작을 당하거나 받는 대상이 중심일 경우에는 수동태를 써야 해요.

수동태는 ‘ ______ ’ 형태로 동사를 만들어요.

2 수동태의 부정문은 be동사 뒤에 ______ 을 써서 표현해요.

3 수동태의 의문문은 ______ 를 문장 맨 앞으로 보내서 만들어요. 대답은 Yes/No로 하고 행위의 대상인 주어에 알맞은 ______ 와 ______ 로 답하면 돼요.

REVIEW TARGET WORDS 주어진 단어의 철자/뜻을 쓰세요.

□ ______	ⓥ (그림을) 그리다	□ picture	ⓝ ______
□ ______	ⓝ 거울	□ invite	ⓥ ______
□ ______	ⓝ 사원	□ destroy	ⓥ ______
□ ______	ⓝ 쌀	□ grow	ⓥ ______
□ ______	ⓥ 고용하다	□ film	ⓝ ______
□ ______	ⓐ 부주의한	□ accident	ⓝ ______
□ ______	ⓝ 소포	□ neighbor	ⓝ ______
□ ______	ⓝ 지갑	□ fix	ⓥ ______
□ ______	ⓥ 배달하다	□ light bulb	______
□ ______	ⓥ 발명하다	□ government	ⓝ ______
□ ______	ⓝ 세금	□ drink	ⓝ ______
□ ______	ⓝ 약, 약품	□ ingredient	ⓝ ______
□ ______	ⓥ (음식물을) 제공하다	□ open	ⓥ ______

unit 08

과거와 현재완료

TARGET WORDS 알고 있는 단어는 check(√) 후 뜻을 쓰고, 모르는 단어는 조사해 오세요 !

☐ anchor	ⓝ ________	☐ hiking	ⓝ ________	☐ headache	ⓝ ________
☐ news	ⓝ ________	☐ ghost	ⓝ ________	☐ delicious	ⓐ ________
☐ history	ⓝ ________	☐ Korean War	________	☐ break out	________
☐ photographer	ⓝ ________	☐ volleyball	ⓝ ________	☐ look for	________
☐ cast	ⓝ ________	☐ fix	ⓥ ________	☐ teenager	ⓝ ________
☐ strange	ⓐ ________	☐ visit	ⓥ ________	☐ waterski	ⓥ ________

unit 08

과거와 현재완료는 어떻게 다른가요?

현재완료는 과거의 행위가 언제 일어났는지 또 언제 했는지 정확하지 않은 시점에 이미 끝난 동작을 나타내요. 반면에, 현재와는 아무런 연관성도 없고, 과거에 구체적인 시점이 언급되면 과거 시제를 써요.

They **went** to Turkey in July, **2001**.
그들은 2001년 7월에 터키에 갔다.

After a month, they **went** to Singapore.
한 달 후에 그들은 싱카포르에 갔다.

과거는 있었던 일만을 나타내고 과거의 시점(in 2001)이라는 특정한 시점을 말할 수 있어요.

Linda **has bought** a new car. (현재완료)
Linda는 새 차를 샀다. (=She **has** a new car **now**.)

현재완료는 과거에 언제 샀는지 보다는 현재의 상태나 행동이 중요하기 때문에 특정한 과거의 시점이 중요하지도 않고 언급하지도 않아요.

Linda **bought** it **last week**. (과거)
Linda는 그것을 지난주에 샀다.

과거의 구체적인 시점을 언급하려면 과거 시제를 써야 해요.

현재완료 계속은 과거부터 현재까지 계속되는 동작이나 상태를 뜻해요. 반면에 과거 시제는 과거에 시작한 일이 과거에 끝났을 때 사용해요.

She **was** a news anchor **for** 5 years.
그녀는 5년 동안 뉴스앵커였다.

She **has been** a news anchor **for** 5 years.
그녀는 5년 동안 뉴스 앵커를 하고 있다.

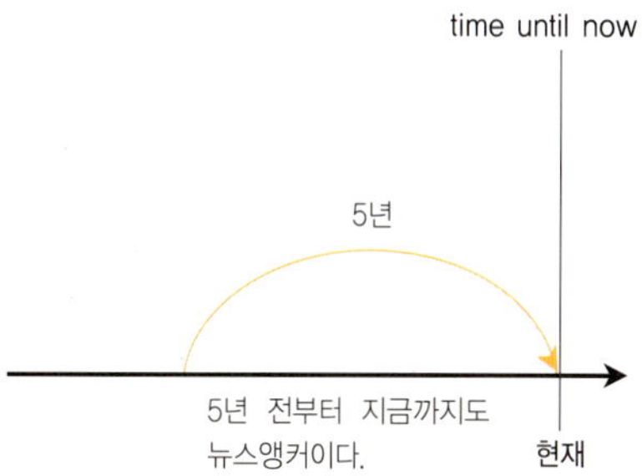

현재완료는 yesterday, ago, last week, in 1999 등과 같이 과거의 특정한 시점을 꼭 집어 말하는 과거표시어구와 함께 쓸 수 없어요. 특히 when과 what time과 함께 쓸 수 없어요.

I **saw** Mary **yesterday**. 나는 어제 Mary를 봤다.

When did they arrive? 그들은 언제 도착했나요?

They **went** to Turkey **in 2003**. 그들은 2003년에 터키에 갔다.

She **watched** TV too late **last night**. 그녀는 지난밤에 TV를 너무 늦게까지 봤다.

과거와 현재완료

01 과거 시제는 어떨때 쓰나요?

과거 시제는 과거에 시작한 일이 [ ] 에 끝났으며 [ ] 와 아무런 관련이 없는 경우에 써요.

과거의 구체적인 시점을 언급하면 과거 시제를 써야 해요.

I **went** hiking two weeks **ago**. 나는 2주전에 하이킹을 하러 갔다.

He **lived** in Seoul for two years. 그는 2년 동안 서울에 살았었다.

02 현재완료는 과거와 무엇이 다르나요?

현재완료는 과거에 시작하여 과거 불특정한 시점에 끝난 행위이거나 과거에 시작한 그 행위나 상태가 현재까지 계속되고 있을 때 사용해요. [ ] 에 그 행위나 상태가 중요하기 때문에 과거의 특정한 시점이 중요하지 않아요.

He **has lived** in Seoul for two years. 그는 2년 동안 서울에 살고 있다. (지금도 살고 있음)

Karen **had** a headache for three hours this morning.
Karen은 오늘 아침 3시간 동안 두통이 있었다. (그녀는 지금 두통이 있지 않다.)

Karen **has had** a headache for three hours.
Karen은 3시간 동안 두통이 있다. (그녀는 아직도 두통이 있다.)

03 현재완료와 함께 못 쓰는 표현이 뭐예요?

현재완료는 지금 현재의 행동이나 상태를 중요하게 생각하기 때문에 과거를 꼭 집어 말하는 과거표시 어구 (in+과거연대, yesterday, ago, last week, when, what time) 등과 함께 쓸 수 없어요.

Did you go to New Zealand **in 2004**? 2004년에 뉴질랜드에 갔나요?

Yesterday, she **told** me about her boyfriend. 어제 그녀는 나에게 그녀의 남자친구에 대해서 말해주었다.

When did you hear the news? 언제 그 뉴스를 들었나요?

Did you see the movie **last Saturday**? 지난 토요일에 영화를 봤니?

unit 08

Exercise 1

1 (　　) 안에 알맞은 시제를 고르세요.

(1) I (finished / have finished) my homework yesterday.

(2) I (finished / have finished) my homework.

(3) Did you (saw / see / seen) the movie last Sunday?

(4) Have you (saw / see / seen) the movie before?

(5) Eun-sun (visited / has visited) Tokyo when she was a student.

(6) Eun-sun (visited / has visited) Tokyo before.

(7) They (saw / have seen) a ghost in 1998.

(8) They (saw / have seen) a ghost twice.

2 (　　) 안의 동사를 적절한 시제로 바꿔 문장을 완성하세요.

(1) Kelly and I are good friends. We ______________ (know) each other for 10 years.

(2) He __________ (read) the book three hours ago.

(3) I have never __________ (eat) such a delicious food.

(4) My history teacher told us that the Korean War __________ (break) out in 1950.

(5) We __________ (live) in Seattle last year.

(6) We ______________ (live) in Seattle for three years.

Unit 08

Exercise 2

주어진 상황에 맞는 동사를 보기 에서 골라 완료시제로 쓰세요.

보기

buy lose play break read be

(1)

Kevin ________________ a photographer for ten years.

(2)

They ________________ beach volleyball since last summer.

(3)

My dad ________________ a newspaper for two hours.

(4)

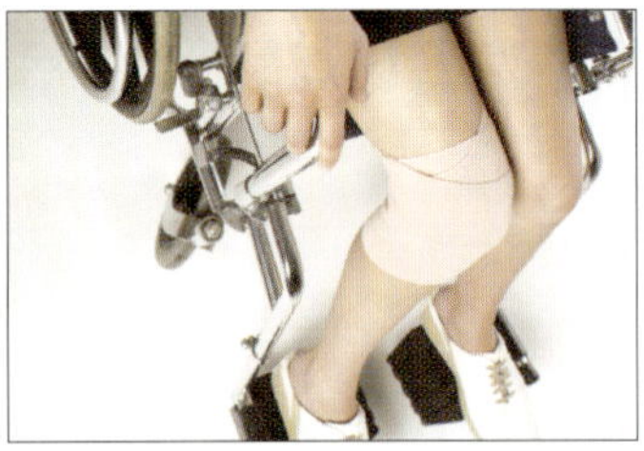

Jane can't walk and her leg is in a cast.
She ________________ her leg.

(5)

He is looking for his key.
He can't find it.
He ________________ his key.

(6)

Nancy ________________ a digital camera.
She ________________ it last week.

unit 08 Exercise 3

빈칸에 주어진 단어를 이용하여 과거 또는 현재완료 시제를 완성하세요.

(1) **A**: I __________ (see) Kevin yesterday.

B: Oh really? I ____________________ (not see) him for a long time.

(2) **A**: How is your computer? __________ you __________ (fix) it?

B: No, I haven't. I'm going to fix it tomorrow.

(3) **A**: What __________ you __________ (do) last Sunday?

B: I __________ (stay) at home.

(4) **A**: __________ you ______________ (finish) your homework yet?

B: Yes, I ______________ (finish) it two hours ago.

(5) **A**: __________ you __________ (be) to Turkey?

B: Yes, I __________ (go) to Turkey last summer.

(6) **A**: __________ you __________ __________ (ever / play) soccer?

B: Yes, I ____________ (play) when I was a teenager.

(7) **A**: What time __________ (do) you __________ (go) to bed last night?

B: I __________ (go) to bed at ten o'clock.

(8) **A**: It's eleven o'clock. Go to bed.

B: Okay. I ____________________________ (just / finish) my homework, so I am going to bed.

unit 08

Jump Up!

1 다음 문장의 빈칸에 알맞은 것을 고르세요.

When __________ to Singapore?

① is he gone ② has he gone ③ did he go
④ was he gone ⑤ did he gone

2 다음 우리말과 같도록 영작할 때 빈칸 a, b에 알맞은 것끼리 짝지은 것은?

A: 선생님에게 너의 숙제에 관해서 벌써 물어봤니?
B: 응, 어제 선생님에게 말했어.
→ **A**: __________ the teacher about your homework yet?
B: Yes, I __________ to her yesterday.

	a	b
①	Did you ask	have talked
②	Have you asked	talked
③	Have you asked	have talked
④	Did you ask	talked
⑤	Have you asked	will talk

3 다음 문장의 빈칸에 알맞은 것을 고르세요.

I have seen a strange woman __________.

① two years ago ② before ③ last week
④ when I was a child ⑤ yesterday

strange ⓐ 이상한, 낯선

Writing Activity

보기 와 같이 주어진 정보를 이용하여 알맞은 의문문과 그 대답을 쓰세요.

보기

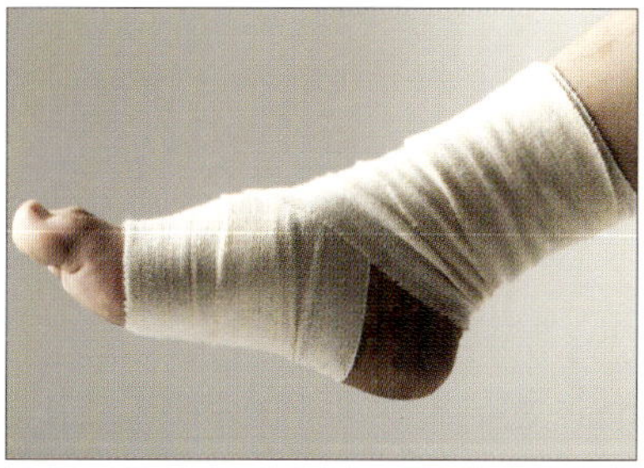

your brother / break / his leg
→ Yes / it / last week

Has your brother broken his leg?
→ Yes, he has. He broke it last week.

(1)

you / ever / visit / Egypt
→ Yes / Egypt / two years ago

______________________?
→ Yes, I ________.
I ______________________.

(2)

you / ever / eat / Korean food
→ Yes / Korean food / yesterday

______________________?
→ Yes, I ________.
I ______________________.

(3)

Sunny / try / waterskiing
→ Yes / waterskiing / last month

______________________?
→ Yes, she ________.
She ______________________.

unit 08

Oral Test!

1 현재완료는 [   ]에 행위나 상태가 남아있거나 계속되고 있다는 뜻을 내포하기 때문에 과거의 특정한 시점이 중요하지도 언급하지도 않아요.

2 과거시제는 [   ]에 시작한 일이 과거에 끝났으며 [   ]와는 전혀 연관이 없는 경우에 써요. 과거의 구체적인 시점이 중요하므로 과거를 나타내는 과거표현과 함께 쓰여요.

3 현재완료는 현재와 깊은 관련이 있기 때문에 과거를 정확히 말해주는 [   ] 표현과는 함께 쓸 수 없어요. 예를 들어, 현재완료는 yesterday, in + 과거연대, last month, when, what time 등과 함께 쓸 수 없어요.

REVIEW TARGET WORDS 주어진 단어의 철자/뜻을 쓰세요.

☐ anchor	ⓝ ________	☐ ________	ⓝ 도보 여행
☐ headache	ⓝ ________	☐ ________	ⓝ 뉴스, 소식
☐ ghost	ⓝ ________	☐ ________	ⓐ 맛있는
☐ history	ⓝ ________	☐ ________	한국 전쟁
☐ break out	________	☐ ________	ⓝ 사진가
☐ volleyball	ⓝ ________	☐ ________	찾다, 구하다
☐ cast	ⓝ ________	☐ ________	ⓥ 고치다
☐ teenager	ⓝ ________	☐ ________	ⓐ 이상한, 낯선
☐ visit	ⓥ ________	☐ ________	ⓥ 수상 스키를 타다

Progress Test 2

✖ ( ) 안에서 알맞은 말을 고르세요. (1~4)

1 They enjoyed (to watch / watching) the movie.

2 It stopped (to rain / raining) a few minutes ago.

3 My dad quit (to smoke / smoking).

4 Would you mind (to close / closing) the window?

✖ 다음 주어진 동사의 과거형과 be+과거분사의 수동형으로 써 보세요. (5~8)

	동사원형	과거형	be+과거분사(수동태)
5	ask	________	be ________
6	know	________	be ________
7	lose	________	be ________
8	write	________	be ________

✖ 주어진 단어를 이용하여 5형식 문장으로 완성하세요. (9~10)

9

"Don't talk!" the teacher said to us. (tell)

➡ The teacher ________________________.

10

"Stay in your car", the police officer said. (order)

➡ The police officer ________________________.

✖ (　) 안에 알맞은 시제를 써 넣으세요. (11~14)

11 Karen (visited / has visited) her uncle yesterday.

12 Lisa (lost / has lost) her book. She can't find it.

13 We (went / has gone) to the movies, but we didn't enjoy the film much.

14 Linda and I are old friends. I (knew / have known) her since I was an elementary school student.

Progress Test 1 Score : (   ) of 20

✖ 주어진 문장을 수동태로 고쳐 다시 쓰세요. (15~16)

15 He finished the work.

➡ ____.

16 Many people read the newspaper.

➡ ____.

✖ 주어진 문장을 지시대로 고쳐 쓰세요. (17~20)

17 The letter was written by Jane. (부정문으로)

➡ ____.

18 Many people saw the accident. (수동태 의문문으로)

➡ ______________________________? No, ______________.

19 Nancy broke the window. (수동태 부정문으로)

➡ ____.

20 Thomas Edison invented the light bulb. (수동태 의문문으로)

➡ ______________________________? Yes, ______________.

unit 09

미래를 나타내는 부사절

TARGET WORDS 알고 있는 단어는 check(√) 후 뜻을 쓰고, 모르는 단어는 조사해 오세요 !

☐ mix	ⓥ ________	☐ plant	ⓝ ________	☐ lose weight	________
☐ airport	ⓝ ________	☐ go fishing	________	☐ driver's licence	________
☐ go out	________	☐ hurry	ⓥ ________	☐ take care of	________
☐ lock	ⓥ ________	☐ job	ⓝ ________	☐ as soon as	________
☐ medicine	ⓝ ________	☐ feel better	________	☐ go for a walk	________
☐ champion	ⓝ ________	☐ tired	ⓐ ________	☐ graduate from	________
☐ retire	ⓥ ________	☐ cloud	ⓝ ________	☐ classical music	________
☐ look for	________	☐ cold	ⓝ ________	☐ get fat	________

unit 09

미래를 나타내는 부사절이 뭐예요?

시간을 나타내는 부사절 (when~, before~, after~)과 조건을 나타내는 부사절 (if~, unless~)에 동사는 현재형이 오지만 표현은 미래를 나타내는 것을 말해요.

When you **mix** red and white, you will get pink.
빨간색과 하얀색을 섞었을 때, 핑크색이 된다.

시간을 나타내는 부사절 안에, 'will+동사원형(will mix)' 대신에 현재 시제(mix)를 써서 미래를 나타내요.

After they **graduate** from university, they will get a good job.
대학을 졸업한 후에, 그들은 좋은 직업을 갖게 될 것이다.

= They will get a good job **after** they **graduate** from university.

미래는 조동사 will과 be going to를 이용해서 표현한다고 배웠지만, 시간의 부사절 안에 있는 동사에는 will이나 be going to를 쓰지 않아요. 단, 주인 문장(주절)에는 미래 시제를 써야 합니다.

어떤 일에 대한 계획표, 예정표 또는 이미 확실히 정해져 있는 일정에는 현재 시제가 미래를 나타내요.

The next plane **leaves** at 10:30 tomorrow.
다음 비행기가 내일 아침 10:30에 떠난다.

The concert **starts** at 7:30.
그 콘서트는 7:30에 시작한다.

현재진행 시제(be + -ing)가 미래의 계획, 개인의 일정, 특정한 시간의 표현과 함께 쓰여 미래를 표현 할 수 있어요.

The next plane **is flying** to Jeju Island in two hours.
다음 비행기가 2시간 안에 제주도로 간다.

조건의 부사절(if~, unless~)은 시간의 부사절과 마찬가지로 현재 시제로 미래를 표현할 수 있어요.

If the weather **is** nice tomorrow, we'll go fishing.
내일 날씨가 좋다면, 우리는 낚시하러 갈 것이다.
= We'll go fishing **if** the weather **is** nice tomorrow.

조건의 부사절에서는 현재 시제가 미래를 대신하고, 주절(주인 문장)에는 미래 시제를 써요.

unless는 If … not의 뜻으로 unless 조건절에는 부정문을 쓰지 않아요.

Unless you **have** a driver's license, you can't drive a car.
운전 면허가 없다면, 당신은 차를 운전할 수 없다.
= **If** you **don't** have a driver's license, you can't drive a car.

Unit 09

미래를 나타내는 부사절

01 시간의 부사절이 미래를 나타낼 수 있나요?

시간의 접속사 when, after, before, as soon as 등의 부사절이 [   ] 시제일 때 그 형태는 현재이지만 미래를 나타내는 표현이 돼요. 주절(주인 문장)에는 미래 시제를 써요.

Before our boss **comes**, I will leave. 사장님이 오기 전에, 나는 떠날 거야.
When it **stops** raining, we'll go out. 비가 그칠 때, 우리는 밖으로 나갈 거야.

02 조건의 부사절이 미래를 나타낼 수 있나요?

조건의 부사절(if~, unless~)에서 [   ] 시제가 미래를 표현해요. 의미가 비록 미래일지라도 미래를 나타내는 will이나 be going to를 쓰지 않아요. 단, 주절(주인 문장)에는 미래 시제를 써요.

If I **have** time tomorrow, I will visit you. 내일 시간이 있다면, 너를 방문할게.

Hurry up! **If** we **don't hurry**, we'll be late. 서둘러! 서두르지 않으면, 우리는 늦을 거야.
=Hurry up! **Unless** we **hurry**, we'll be late.

Let's go to the movies **if** you **aren't** too tired. 네가 너무 피곤하지 않다면, 영화 보러 가자.
=Let's go to the movies **unless** you **are** too tired.

03 현재 시제와 진행형 시제도 미래를 표현 하나요?

확정된 일정, 또는 계획표, 예정표와 같은 일에는 현재 시제가 미래를 나타낼 수 있어요.
현재진행 시제는 이미 결정된 일, 또는 개인의 일정, 특정한 시간의 표현과 함께 미래를 표현할 수 있어요.

I **am bringing** some juice to the party. 나는 그 파티에 쥬스를 가져갑니다.
The movie **begins** in 5 minutes. 영화가 5분 안에 시작할 거야.
The train **arrives** at 10:30 tomorrow. 열차가 내일 10:30에 도착할 거야.

unit 09

Exercise 1

( ) 안에서 알맞은 시제를 고르세요.

(1) After I (do / did) my homework tonight, I'm going to go to bed.

(2) After I (do / did) my homework last night, I went to bed.

(3) Before Kevin (leaves / left) for work this morning, he locked the door.

(4) Before Kevin (leaves / left) for work this morning, he's going to lock the door.

(5) I'll call you after I (get / got) home this evening.

(6) **A**: What time will you phone me tomorrow?
B: I'll call you when I (get / got) home from work.

(7) We'll go out when it (stops / stopped) raining.

(8) If you (don't eat / didn't eat) less, you won't lose weight.

(9) I'll stay inside if it (rains / rained).

(10) If the weather (is / was) nice tomorrow, we'll go hiking.

(11) Class will begin as soon as the teacher (arrives / arrived).

(12) We (go / went) for a walk when the rain stopped.

(13) I will tell him the news as soon as I (see / saw) him.

(14) If you (lie / lied) to me, I will tell your sister about it.

(15) He will be here before you (go / went).

unit 09 Exercise 2

| 다음 주어진 정보를 이용하여 현재진행형 시제로 미래를 표현해 보세요.

(1) 

play tennis / on Saturday

Peter ______________________.

(2) 

have dinner / with Bob

Lisa ______________________.

(3) 

go / to the movies / tonight

Jason ______________________.

(4) 

go / to a party

Laura and Kelly ______________

______________________.

2 다음 주어진 조건의 부사절 안의 시제를 알맞은 형태로 바꾸세요.

(1) If you ________ (take) your medicine, you'll feel better.

(2) If he ________ (work) hard, he'll pass the exam.

(3) If they ________ (win) the game, they will be champions.

(4) If it ________ (rain) tonight, I will stay at home.

Unit 09 Exercise 3

보기 와 같이 주어진 접속사를 이용하여 문장을 쓰세요.

보기

You wake him up.
He will cry.

If you wake him up, he will cry.

(1)

You travel to Korea.
You will meet some nice people.

If you ______________________,
you ______________________.

(2)

You water the plants.
They won't die.

If you ______________________,
they ______________________.

(3)

Linda listens to classical music.
Then, she will go to bed tonight.

Before Linda ____________ tonight,
she will ______________________.

unit 09

Jump Up!

주어진 문장을 읽고 제시된 접속사를 이용하여 문장을 완성하시오.

(1) I will retire. I will play tennis. (when)

➡ ______________________________.

(2) I will be old. I will take care of myself. (when)

➡ ______________________________.

(3) He will finish his homework. He's going to go to bed. (after)

➡ __________ his homework, __________.

(4) Ann will finish her homework. She will watch TV tonight. (before)

➡ __________ TV tonight, __________ her homework.

(5) I will call Bob tomorrow. I'll ask him to come to my party. (when)

➡ __________ Bob tomorrow, __________ to my party.

(6) Kelly will get home tonight. She's going to read the history book. (after)

➡ __________ the history book __________ home tonight .

(7) Sunny will graduate. She will look for a job. (when)

➡ ______________________________ a job.

(8) I will be 25 years old. I will get married. (when)

➡ ______________________________ married.

retire ⓥ 은퇴(퇴직)하다
take care of ~을 돌보다
go to bed 잠자리에 들다
graduate ⓥ 졸업하다
look for ~을 찾다, 구하다
job ⓝ 직업

unit 09

Writing Activity

1 보기 에 주어진 단어를 이용하여 현재 시제가 미래를 나타낼 수 있도록 빈칸을 영작하세요.

보기		
open	begin	leave

(1) **A**: What time ________ the class ________ tomorrow morning?

B: It ________ at seven o'clock.

(2) The movie theater ________ at seven o'clock tomorrow morning. I'll meet Kathy there at 8:00.

(3) **A**: What time are you going to go to the Seoul station tonight?

B: Bob's train ________ around 7:30, but I think I'll go a little early.

2 Jason은 집과 떨어져 수학여행을 가고 있어요. Jason의 엄마는 걱정을 많이 하고 있답니다. 엄마가 Jason에게 해 주는 말을 영작해 보세요. (if를 사용해서 영작하세요.)

(1) go out without a coat / get a cold

➡ ________________________________.

(2) don't eat breakfast / be hungry

➡ ________________________________.

(3) eat too many chocolates / get fat

➡ ________________________________.

(4) go to bed early / not be tired the next day

➡ ________________________________.

unit 09

Oral Test!

1 시간의 접속사 when, after, before, as soon as의 부사절에서 동사는 [ ] 를 써서 미래를 나타내요. 그 의미가 미래를 나타낼지라도 부사절 안에 [ ] 같은 미래 시제를 쓰지 않아요.

2 조건의 부사절 (if ~, unless ~) 안에도 마찬가지로 [ ] 가 미래를 대신해요. 단, 주절(주인 문장)에는 [ ] 시제를 써야 해요.

3 개인의 확정된 일정 또는 예정표와 같은 일에는 [ ] 나 [ ] 으로도 미래를 나타낼 수 있어요.

REVIEW TARGET WORDS 주어진 단어의 철자/뜻을 쓰세요.

□ mix	ⓥ ________	□ ________	~을 졸업하다
□ job	ⓝ ________	□ ________	ⓝ 공항
□ go fishing	________	□ ________	운전면허증
□ go out	________	□ ________	ⓥ 서두르다
□ cloud	ⓝ ________	□ ________	ⓥ 잠그다
□ lose weight	________	□ ________	~하자마자
□ go for a walk	________	□ ________	ⓝ 약
□ feel better	________	□ ________	ⓝ 우승자, 챔피언
□ tired	ⓐ ________	□ ________	ⓝ 식물
□ classical music	________	□ ________	ⓥ 은퇴하다
□ take care of	________	□ ________	~을 찾다, 구하다
□ cold	ⓝ ________	□ ________	살찌다

unit 10

관계대명사 1

TARGET WORDS 알고 있는 단어는 check(√) 후 뜻을 쓰고, 모르는 단어는 조사해 오세요!

☐ dentist	ⓝ ________	☐ next door	________	☐ friendly	ⓐ ________
☐ worth	ⓐ ________	☐ healthy	ⓐ ________	☐ fresh	ⓐ ________
☐ apply	ⓥ ________	☐ be interested in	________	☐ climb	ⓥ ________
☐ ending	ⓝ ________	☐ be covered with	________	☐ injure	ⓥ ________
☐ saw	ⓝ ________	☐ every half hour	________	☐ biography	ⓝ ________
☐ uncle	ⓝ ________	☐ direction	ⓝ ________	☐ tool	ⓝ ________
☐ attract	ⓥ ________	☐ tourist	ⓝ ________	☐ lay	ⓥ ________
☐ scientific	ⓐ ________	☐ research	ⓝ ________	☐ special	ⓐ ________
☐ animal	ⓝ ________	☐ ostrich	ⓝ ________	☐ star in	________
☐ popular	ⓐ ________	☐ huge	ⓐ ________	☐ statue	ⓝ ________
☐ painter	ⓝ ________	☐ navigation	ⓝ ________		

Unit 10

관계대명사가 뭐예요?

관계대명사란 관계시켜주면서 대명사 역할을 한다는 것을 의미해요. 앞서 대명사에 대해서 공부를 했어요.

I know **a girl**.
나는 한 소녀를 안다.

She plays the violin well.
그녀는 바이올린을 잘 켠다.

위의 그림에서 She는 누구의 대명사인가요?? 그렇죠! a girl을 대명사 she로 받은 거예요. 그렇다면 "She plays the violin well."에서 대명사 She 말고 또 다른 대명사로 "Who(그녀는) plays the violin well."이라고 말하면 이번에는 Who가 a girl이라는 것을 알 수 있나요? Who도 She처럼 똑같은 대명사 역할을 할 수 있어요.
단, she는 단지 명사만을 대신 할 뿐 그 이상의 역할을 할 수 없고, 대명사 who는 a girl이라는 명사를 대신하는 대명사 역할도 하고 앞서 말한 문장(I know a girl.)과 함께 연결까지 시켜줄 수 있는 역할까지 할 수 있어요.

I know **a girl**. ⊕ **She** plays the violin well.
주어
↓
Who (주어 She를 대명사 who로 바꿈)

I know **a girl**. **Who** plays the violin well.

→ I know *a girl* **who** plays the violin well.
나는 바이올린을 잘 켜는 소녀를 안다.

대명사 who는 원래는 a girl이었어요. 그래서 두 개를 함께 써서 문장을 연결시키면

I know **a girl a girl** plays the violin well.

이렇게 되죠. 그러면 똑같은 명사 2개가 충돌이 되므로 둘 중 하나를 대명사 who(=a girl)로 바꿔 써서 문장까지 연결시켜 주는 관계대명사가 탄생하게 되었답니다.

관계대명사 앞에 나오는 말을 선행사라고 하는데 a girl who plays the violin처럼 "바이올린을 켜는 소녀" 즉 꾸밈을 받는 명사 'a girl'이 who 앞에 있다고 하여 선행사라는 용어를 써요. 모든 관계대명사는 앞에 있는 선행사(명사)를 꾸며주면서 우리말 '~하는/~할/~했던+명사'로 해석해주면 돼요. 명사를 꾸며준다고 해서 '형용사절'이란 문법 용어도 쓴답니다.

주어가 사람이면 who를 쓰고 주어가 사물이나 동물이면 which를 써요. 즉 선행사가 사람이냐 사물/동물이냐에 따라 who와 which를 구별해서 써야 해요. 단 that은 모든 선행사에 다 쓸 수 있어요. 주어를 대신 했다고 해서 주격 관계대명사라 불러요.

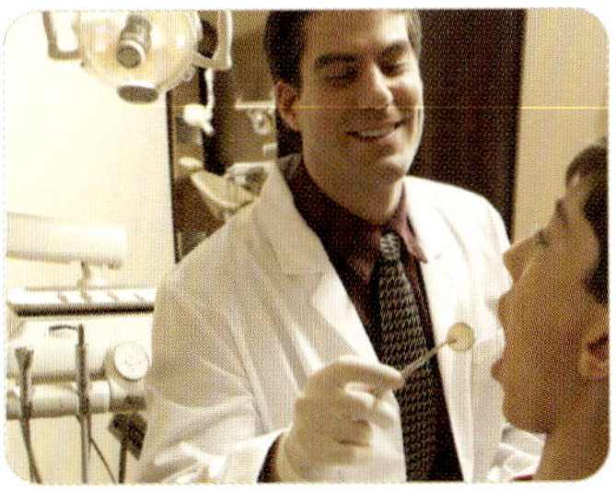

The man is a dentist. ⊕ **He** lives next door.

↓

Who(주어를 대명사 처리 → 주격 관계대명사)

The man is a dentist. **Who** lives next door.

➡ *The man* **who** lives next door is a dentist.
옆집에 사는 그 남자는 치과 의사이다.

Those books are mine. 저 책들은 내꺼야. ⊕ **They** are on the desk. 책은 책상 위에 있어.

➡ *Those books* **which** are on the desk are mine. 책상 위에 있는 책들은 나의 것이야.

관계대명사가 이끄는 형용사절 속의 동사는 선행사가 단수이면 단수동사, 복수이면 복수동사를 써야 해요.

The woman who **lives** next door **is** friendly. 옆집에 사는 여자는 친절하다.

The women who **live** next door **are** friendly. 옆집에 사는 여자들은 친절하다.

관계대명사를 써서 명사를 꾸며주는 이유는 한 문장 안에 있는 특정한 명사를 더욱 구체적으로 보충·설명해 주는 역할을 해요. 즉, 관계대명사가 이끄는 형용사절에 의해 선행사(명사)는 그 의미가 더 구체적으로 설명되는 거예요.

Unit 10

관계대명사 I

01 관계대명사가 뭐예요?

관계대명사는 he, she, it, they와 마찬가지로 명사를 대신해서 쓰는 (   )예요. 그런데 보통의 대명사와의 차이점은 문장과 문장을 연결시켜 줄 수 있는 역할까지 겸하고 있어서 관계대명사라고 불러요.

He is **a boy**. 그는 소년이다. + **He** helped me. 그는 나를 도와주었다.

→ He is a boy. Who helped me.

→ He is *a boy* **who** help me. 그는 나를 도와준 소년이다.

02 who, which, that은 어떻게 구별해서 쓰나요?

who는 선행사가 (   ) 일 때, which는 선행사가 (   ) / (   ) 일 때 써요. 그리고 that은 선행사가 그 무엇이든 관계없이 모두 쓸 수 있어요.

I have *a friend* **who** lives in Mexico. 나는 멕시코에 살고 있는 친구가 있다.

=I have *a friend* **that** lives in Mexico.

This is *a book* **which** is worth reading. 이 책은 읽어 볼 만한 가치가 있는 책이야.

=This is *a book* **that** is worth reading.

03 주격 관계대명사가 뭐예요?

주격이란 주어 자격이란 말이에요. 즉, 관계대명사가 문장안의 (   )를 대신했을 때 주격 관계대명사라고 하는 거예요.

04 관계대명사 안에 있는 동사의 단·복수는 어떻게 구별해요?

관계대명사가 이끄는 형용사절 속의 동사는 선행사가 단수이면 (   )동사, 복수이면 (   )동사를 써야 해요.

The book which **is** on the table **is** hers. 책상 위에 있는 그 책은 그녀의 것이다.

The books which **are** on the table **are** hers. 책상 위에 있는 그 책들은 그녀의 것이다.

unit 10

Exercise 1

( ) 안에서 알맞은 관계대명사를 고르세요.

(1) A person (who / which) drinks a lot of water is healthy.

(2) Food (who / which) is fresh is good for you.

(3) The woman (who / which) lives next door is a dancer.

(4) Anyone (who / which) is interested in the job must apply before next Friday.

(5) Pandas are animals (who / which) can climb trees.

(6) This is the actor (who / which) won the Oscar last year.

(7) I don't like movies (who / which) have unhappy endings.

(8) Look at the house (who / which) is covered with snow.

(9) This is the man (who / which) saved her life.

(10) Where is the letter (who / which) arrived yesterday?

(11) The girl (who / which) was injured in the accident is now in the hospital.

(12) I saw the people (who / which) were playing soccer at the park.

(13) The park (who / which) is near my house is good.

(14) The students (who / which) make lots of noise are Kevin and Tom.

(15) I saw your brother (who / which) didn't say hello to me.

unit 10

Exercise 2

1 (   ) 안에서 알맞은 단수/복수동사를 고르세요.

(1) The women who (was / were) sitting in front of me made lots of noise.

(2) Look at the boy who (is / are) playing with the ball.

(3) I have a dog which (has / have) black spots.

(4) A saw is a tool that (is / are) used to cut wood.

(5) I met a man who (live / lives) in Mexico.

(6) A book that (tells / tell) the story of a person's life is called a biography.

(7) I talked to the men who (was / were) sitting near me.

(8) I have an uncle who (works / work) at the post office.

(9) Do you know the people that (lives / live) in that house?

2 표시된 명사를 who 또는 which로 바꿔 한 문장으로 만드세요.

(1) Do you know the people? **They** live in Seoul.
→ Do you know the people ______________________________?

(2) The officer was friendly. **He** gave me directions.
→ The officer ______________________________ was friendly.

(3) The bus goes to the airport. **It** runs every half hour.
→ The bus ______________________________ goes to the airport.

(4) I like houses. **They** have many windows.
→ I like houses ______________________________.

Exercise 3

1 (　　) 안에 알맞은 것을 고르세요.

(1) The woman (who / which) (live / lives) next to me has four puppies.

(2) Seoul is a city (who / which) (attract / attracts) tourists.

(3) Someone (who / which) (have / has) a lot of friends is lucky.

(4) I have a girlfriend (who / which) (love / loves) to shop.

(5) New York is a city (who / which) never (sleep / sleeps).

(6) These are the geese (who / which) (lay / lays) golden eggs.

(7) I hate the girl (who / which) (talk / talks) too much.

2 (　　) 안에 주어진 말을 이용하여 관계대명사 who나 which가 들어간 문장을 완성하세요.

(1)

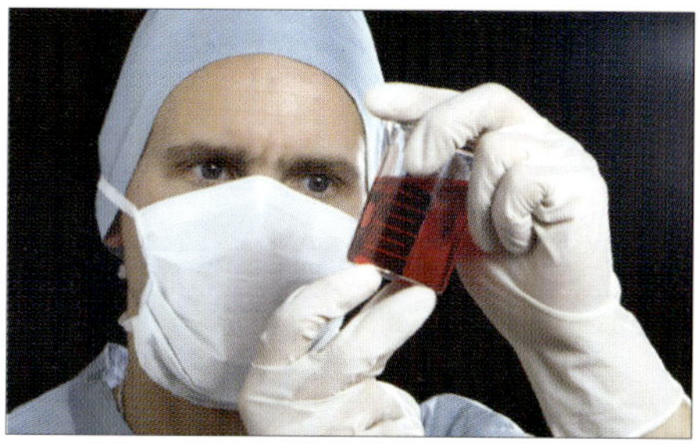

A scientist is someone

______________________________.

(do some scientific research)

(2)

A bee is an insect

______________________________.

(make honey)

unit 10

Jump Up!

다음 주어진 문장을 관계대명사 who나 which를 이용하여 한 문장으로 만드세요.

(1) Australia is a country. ⊕ It has some special animals.

➡ ______________________________

______________________________.

(2) Kangaroos are animals. ⊕ They live in Australia.

➡ ______________________________.

(3) An ostrich is a bird. ⊕ It doesn't fly.

➡ ______________________________.

(4) An orange is a fruit. ⊕ It has a lot of vitamin C.

➡ ______________________________

______________________________.

(5) Do you know the man? ⊕ He took care of animals in his life.

➡ ______________________________

______________________________?

(6) The Beatles were four young men. ⊕
These young men became famous all over the world.

➡ ______________________________

______________________________.

(7) Brad Pitt is an actor. ⊕ This actor stars in a lot of popular movies.

➡ ______________________________

______________________________.

(8) James Dean was an actor. ⊕ This actor died young.

➡ ______________________________.

(9) The Sphinx is a huge statue. ⊕ It is near the pyramids.

➡ ______________________________

______________________________.

special
ⓐ 특별한, 특이한
animal ⓝ 동물
ostrich ⓝ 타조
take care of
~을 돌보다
all over the world
전 세계에서
star in
(영화에서) 주연하다
popular ⓐ 인기 있는
actor ⓝ (남자) 배우
Sphinx
ⓝ 스핑크스 (인간 또는 동물의 머리와 사자의 몸으로 된 석상)
huge
ⓐ 거대한, 매우 큰
statue ⓝ 조각상

Writing Activity

( ) 안에 주어진 말을 이용하여 관계대명사 who나 which가 들어간 문장을 완성하세요.

(1)

A painter is someone

________________________________.

(draw / pictures)

(2)

Navigation is something ____________

________________ when you're lost.

(help / you / find / your way)

(3)

A firefighter is a person ____________

________________________________.

(save / people's lives)

(4)

Manchester United is the soccer team

____

________________________________.

(win / the Champions League / last year)

Oral Test!

1 관계대명사는 보통의 대명사인 he, she, it과 같은 [　　　　] 예요. 그러나 가장 큰 차이점은, 관계대명사는 [　　　　] 과 [　　　　] 을 연결시켜 줄 수 있는 역할까지 겸하고 있다는 거예요.

2 선행사가 사람 일 때는 [　　　　] 를 쓰고, 선행사가 사물 또는 동물 일 때는 [　　　　] 를 써야 해요. [　　　　] 은 사람, 사물, 동물 그 어떤 선행사에도 다 쓸 수 있는 관계대명사예요.

3 관계대명사가 주어를 대명사 처리 했을 경우 이를 [　　　　] 관계대명사라고 해요.

4 관계대명사가 이끄는 형용사절 속의 동사는 선행사가 단수이면 [　　　　] 동사, 복수이면 [　　　　] 동사를 써야 해요.

REVIEW TARGET WORDS 주어진 단어의 철자/뜻을 쓰세요.

☐ dentist	ⓝ ________	☐ ________		옆집에 (사는)
☐ friendly	ⓐ ________	☐ ________	ⓐ	가치가 있는
☐ healthy	ⓐ ________	☐ ________	ⓐ	신선한
☐ be interested in	________	☐ ________	ⓥ	지원하다
☐ climb	ⓥ ________	☐ ________	ⓝ	결말, 끝
☐ be covered with	________	☐ ________	ⓥ	다치게 하다
☐ saw	ⓝ ________	☐ ________	ⓝ	도구
☐ biography	ⓝ ________	☐ ________	ⓝ	삼촌
☐ direction	ⓝ ________	☐ ________		30분마다
☐ attract	ⓥ ________	☐ ________	ⓝ	관광객, 여행자
☐ lay	ⓥ ________	☐ ________	ⓐ	과학(적인)의
☐ reserch	ⓝ ________	☐ ________	ⓐ	특별한, 특이한
☐ animal	ⓝ ________	☐ ________	ⓝ	타조
☐ star in	________	☐ ________	ⓐ	인기 있는
☐ huge	ⓐ ________	☐ ________	ⓝ	조각상
☐ painter	ⓝ ________	☐ ________	ⓝ	항해, 비행, 항공

Unit 11

관계대명사 2

TARGET WORDS 알고 있는 단어는 check(√) 후 뜻을 쓰고, 모르는 단어는 조사해 오세요!

- ☐ funny ⓐ ________
- ☐ happen ⓥ ________
- ☐ movie star ________
- ☐ magician ⓝ ________
- ☐ relax ⓥ ________
- ☐ trust ⓥ ________
- ☐ voice ⓝ ________
- ☐ perfect ⓐ ________
- ☐ touching ⓐ ________
- ☐ shocking ⓐ ________
- ☐ fit ⓥ ________
- ☐ farm ⓝ ________
- ☐ unfortunately ⓐⓓ ________
- ☐ draw ⓥ ________
- ☐ magazine ⓝ ________
- ☐ hate ⓥ ________
- ☐ steal ⓥ ________
- ☐ honesty ⓝ ________
- ☐ attend ⓥ ________
- ☐ own ⓥ ________
- ☐ fantastic ⓐ ________
- ☐ hat ⓝ ________
- ☐ cancel ⓥ ________
- ☐ visit ⓥ ________

unit 11

관계대명사가 뭐예요?

관계대명사는 (대)명사를 대신 할 수 있는 대명사라고 배웠어요. 이번에는 문장에서 목적어를 대신하는 관계대명사를 배우는데, 목적어를 대신 한다고 해서 목적격 관계대명사라고 불러요.

관계대명사 who(m)는 선행사가 사람이고 문장에서 목적어 대신 써요. whom 대신 who나 that으로 많이 쓰고 일상회화에서는 특히 생략하는 것이 자연스러워요.

That is the **funny woman**. ⊕ We met **her** yesterday.
저 사람은 재미있는 여자이다. 우리는 어제 그녀를 만났다.

who(m)
(목적어 her를 대명사 who(m)으로 바꿈)

We met **who(m)** yesterday.

Who(m) we met yesterday.

➡ That is the *funny woman* **who(m)** we met yesterday.
그녀가 어제 우리가 만났던 재미있는 여자이다.
(=That is the funny woman we met yesterday.)

which는 선행사가 사물이나 동물일 때 사용하고 이것 역시 문장 안에서 목적어를 대신하는 목적격 관계대명사예요. 마찬가지로 생략해서 쓰는 것이 훨씬 더 자연스러워요.

The movie was so touching. ⊕ We watched **it** last night.
그 영화는 정말 감동적이었다. 우리는 어제 그것을 보았다.

➡ *The movie* **which (that)** we watched last night was so touching.
우리가 어제 본 영화는 정말 감동적이었다.
(=The movie we watched last night was so touching.)

목적어를 대신해서 사용하는 목적격 관계대명사는 언제든지 생략해서 사용해요.
단, 주격 관계대명사는 생략할 수 없다는 것도 꼭 알아두세요.

대명사 중에 소유격 대명사가 있어요. 아시다시피 소유격은 뒤에 명사가 없으면 문장에서 아무런 역할을 할 수가 없다는 것을 이미 배웠을 거예요(my book 내 책, her book 그녀의 책, his book 그의 책). 마찬가지로 소유격 관계대명사인 whose는 my, her, his와 같이 '~ 의+명사'와 같은 역할을 해요. 보통의 소유격과의 다른 점은 소유격 my, her, his의 역할도 하고 문장까지도 연결시켜 줄 수 있다는 점에서 관계대명사라고 부르는 거예요.

The girl called the police. ⊕ **Her** book was stolen.
그 소녀는 경찰을 불렀다 그녀의 책이 도난당했다.

whose book
(소유격 her를 대명사 whose로 바꿈)

Whose book was stolen.

→ *The girl* **whose book** was stolen called the police.
책을 도난당한 그 소녀는 경찰을 불렀다.

소유격 관계대명사 whose는 선행사가 사람이든 사물이든 모두에 사용하고, whose는 생략할 수 없어요.

관계대명사 what은 선행사를 포함하고 있어서 유일하게 what 앞에 선행사인 명사가 없어요. 우리말 '~것'의 의미이고 the thing that (which)과 같아요.

The thing that happened last night was really shocking.

What happened last night was really shocking.
어제 발생했던 것은 정말 충격적이었다.

The thing that I like about her is her honesty.

What I like about her is her honesty.
내가 그녀에 대해 좋아하는 것은 그녀의 정직함이다.

Unit 11

관계대명사 2

01 목적격 관계대명사가 뭐예요?

1 관계대명사 who(m)는 선행사가 ______ 일 때 문장에서 ______ 대신 써요. whom 대신 who나 that으로 많이 쓰고 특히 일상회화에서는 생략하는 것이 자연스러워요.

She is *the girl* **who(m)** Peter likes. (formal) 그녀는 Peter가 좋아하는 소녀이다.

= She is the girl Peter likes. (informal)

2 which는 선행사가 ______ 이나 ______ 일 때 사용하고 문장 안에서 ______ 를 대신하는 목적격 관계대명사에요. 마찬가지로 생략해서 쓰는 것이 훨씬 더 자연스러워요.

The cellphone **which** Karen bought has a DMB player in it. (formal)
Karen이 산 휴대폰에는 DMB가 내장되어 있다.

= The cellphone Karen bought has a DMB player in it. (informal)

02 소유격 관계대명사가 뭐예요?

my, her, his, their과 같이 소유격 대명사 역할도 하고 문장까지 연결시켜 줄 수 있는 ______ 를 소유격 관계대명사라고 해요. 우리말 '~의(whose) + 명사'와 같은 역할이에요.

I know a girl. + **Her** father is a movie star.

→ I know *a girl* **whose** father is a movie star. 난 아버지가 영화배우인 소녀를 안다.

03 what은 어떨 때 쓰는 거예요?

관계대명사 what은 ______ 를 포함하고 있어서 유일하게 what 앞에 선행사인 ______ 가 없어요. 우리말 '~것'의 의미이고 the thing that(which)과 같아요.

This is **the thing which** I wanted to have.

→ This is **what** I wanted to have. 이것이 내가 가지고 싶어했던 것이다.

unit 11

Exercise 1

( ) 안에서 알맞은 관계대명사를 고르세요.

(1) Have you found the keys (who / that) you lost?

(2) The dress (whose / which) Kelly bought doesn't fit her very well.

(3) The man (who / whose) car was stolen called the police.

(4) The high school (what / that) she attended is in New York.

(5) That is the computer (which / whose) I bought last week.

(6) I met a girl (which / whose) brother is a magician.

(7) I have a friend (who / whom) lives in Singapore.

(8) (What / Which) I need is your love.

(9) I know a man (whom / whose) family is in Egypt.

(10) Don't tell my parents (who / what) I said.

(11) We must ask someone (what / who) knows the way.

(12) The farm (which / whose) my grandfather owns is a great place to relax.

(13) I have lost the watch (what / which) my dad bought for me.

(14) Can you believe (whose / what) they are talking about?

(15) She is married to the man (whom / whose) face is long.

Unit 11

Exercise 2

다음 주어진 문장을 읽고 주격은 who, 목적격은 whom을 써서 문장을 완성해보세요.

(1) That's the man. I met him last year.

➡ That's the man __________ I met last year.

(2) She's the one. She had a lot of money.

➡ She's the one __________ had a lot of money.

(3) Unfortunately, he wasn't the man. I wanted to marry him.

➡ Unfortunately, he wasn't the man __________ I wanted to marry.

(4) My mom had a cook. He made fantastic food.

➡ My mom had a cook __________ made fantastic food.

(5) My friend Jason is a person. I can trust him.

➡ My friend Jason is a person __________ I can trust.

(6) She is the model. I saw her on TV.

➡ She is the model __________ I saw on TV.

(7) Do you know the people? They live in the White House.

➡ Do you know the people __________ live in the White House?

(8) The children were playing basketball. We watched them in the park.

➡ The children __________ we watched in the park were playing basketball.

(9) Jennifer has four sons. They became laywers.

➡ Jennifer has four sons __________ became laywers.

Unit 11 Exercise 3

1 생략할 수 있는 목적격 관계대명사에는 X, 생략할 수 없을 때는 알맞은 관계대명사를 쓰세요.

(1) The picture __________ he drew is very interesting.

(2) The people __________ I met at the party last night were friendly.

(3) A person _______________ drinks a lot of milk is healthy.

(4) I thanked the woman _______________ helped me move the desk.

(5) That man __________ I saw was wearing a black hat.

2 whose를 이용하여 문장을 완성하세요.

(1) 

My brother is a soccer player.

→ I met a boy ______________________________.

(2) 

My dream is to go to Korea.

→ I met a woman ___________________________.

(3) 

My puppy died.

→ I met a girl ______________________________.

unit 11

Jump Up!

1 두 문장을 관계대명사 what을 이용하여 한 문장으로 만드세요.

(1) My girlfriend gave me the thing. I wanted it.

➡ ________________________________.

(2) He'll do anything. He can do that for her.

➡ ________________________________.

2 빈칸에 쓸 수 있는 것을 모두 고르세요.

(1) I really enjoyed the movie ________ we saw last night.

① who ② 생략 가능 ③ which ④ whose

(2) I hear someone ________ voice is beautiful.

① which ② 생략 가능 ③ whose ④ that

(3) The magazine ________ I read on the plane was interesting.

① 생략 가능 ② which ③ what ④ that

voice ⓝ 목소리
magazine ⓝ 잡지

3 다음 두 문장을 하나의 문장으로 연결 할 때 빈칸에 알맞은 것을 고르세요.

This is the thing. ⊕ I wanted to buy it.
➡ This is ________ I wanted to buy.

① who ② which ③ whom ④ that ⑤ what

unit 11

Writing Activity

1 주어진 두 문장을 관계대명사를 이용하여 한 문장으로 만드세요.

(1) Have you found the books? You lost the books.

➡ ______________________________?

(2) I like the dress. Sunny is wearing a dress.

➡ ______________________________.

(3) The airplane was on time. I took the airplane to Nigeria.

➡ ______________________________.

(4) The teacher canceled her English class. The teacher was ill.

➡ ______________________________.

(5) Those are the girls. Their Korean is almost perfect.

➡ ______________________________.

2 관계대명사가 쓰인 각 문장을 두 문장으로 나눠 쓰세요.

(1) Albert Einstein was a boy who hated school.

➡ ______________________________.

➡ ______________________________.

(2) The people whom Nancy visited yesterday were Korean.

➡ ______________________________.

➡ ______________________________.

(3) The strange woman that we saw at the park last night was a ghost.

➡ ______________________________.

➡ ______________________________.

Oral Test!

1 목적격 관계대명사는 관계대명사가 문장에서 [   ]를 대명사 처리하는 거예요. 목적격 관계대명사는 언제나 [   ] 할 수 있어요

2 who(m)는 선행사가 [   ]일 때 사용하고 which는 선행사가 [   ]이나 [   ]일 때 사용해요. that은 어떤 선행사든 관계없이 모두 쓸 수 있어요.

3 my, her, his, their과 같이 소유격 대명사 역할도 하고 문장까지 연결시켜 줄 수 있는 [   ]를 소유격 관계대명사라고 해요. 우리말 '~의(whose)+명사'와 같은 역할이에요.

4 유일하게 선행사를 포함하고 있어서 선행사(명사)와 함께 쓰이지 않는 관계대명사는 [   ]이에요. 우리말 '~것'의 의미이고 [   ]으로 바꿔 쓸 수 있어요.

REVIEW TARGET WORDS 주어진 단어의 철자/뜻을 쓰세요.

☐ ________	ⓐ 우스운	☐ touching	ⓐ ________
☐ ________	ⓥ 훔치다	☐ happen	ⓥ ________
☐ ________	ⓐ 충격적인	☐ honesty	ⓝ ________
☐ ________	영화배우	☐ fit	ⓐ ________
☐ ________	ⓥ (학교 등에) 다니다	☐ magician	ⓝ ________
☐ ________	ⓝ 농장, 농원	☐ own	ⓥ ________
☐ ________	ⓥ 쉬다	☐ unfortunately	ⓐⓓ ________
☐ ________	ⓐ 환상적인, 멋진	☐ trust	ⓥ ________
☐ ________	ⓥ (그림을) 그리다	☐ hat	ⓝ ________
☐ ________	ⓝ 목소리	☐ magazine	ⓝ ________
☐ ________	ⓥ 취소하다	☐ perfect	ⓐ ________
☐ ________	ⓥ 싫어하다	☐ visit	ⓥ ________

Progress Test 3

✖ (　) 안에서 알맞은 말을 고르세요. (1~5)

1 I met Miss Williams who (is / are) a lawyer.

2 We go to a doctor (he / who) has a clinic nearby.

3 Kelly talked to the (worker / workers) who were resting.

4 I know a woman who (makes / making) the loveliest wedding cakes.

5 Justin is a man (he loves / who loves) old songs.

✖ 다음 주어진 상황에 맞게 if로 시작하는 부사절로 문장을 완성하세요. (6~8)

6 

Maybe it will rain tomorrow.

➡ ______________________________, we're going to go to a movie.

7 

Maybe Seo-yoon will have enough time.

➡ ______________________________, she will finish her homework tonight.

8 

Maybe they won't study tonight.

➡ ______________________________, they won't pass the exam.

※ (   ) 안에서 알맞은 관계대명사를 고르세요. (9~12)

9 The dress (whose / which) Sunny bought doesn't fit her very well.

10 I met a girl (who / whose) father is a magician.

11 We must ask someone (what / who) knows the answer.

12 This is (which / what) I wanted to have.

※ 다음 그림을 보기 에 있는 단어들을 이용해서 관계대명사가 들어간 문장으로 완성하세요. (13~16)

13 
14 
15 
16 

보기

fix old cars	cook food in the restaurants
take care of the sick people	take pictures

13 I'm a person ____________________.

14 I'm a person ____________________.

15 I'm a person ____________________.

16 I'm a person ____________________.

Progress Test 3 Score : (   ) of 20

✖ 주어진 문장을 읽고 제시된 접속사를 이용하여 문장을 완성하세요. (17~20)

17 I will retire. I will play golf. (when)

➡ ____.

18 Nancy will finish her homework. She's going to watch TV tonight. (after)

➡ ____.

19 Kelly will go to bed. She's going to finish her work. (before)

➡ ____.

20 We will call Peter tomorrow. We'll ask him to our party. (when)

➡ ____.

Final Test

✖ 주어진 보기 를 이용하여 빈칸에 알맞은 부정사의 표현을 넣으세요. (1~4)

보기

have　　show　　ask　　wish

1

We hold our nose ____________ that something smells bad.

2

We cross our middle and index fingers ____________ good luck.

3

We put a finger to our mouth ____________ for quiet.

4

We go to the cafeteria ____________ some lunch.

5 다음 중 밑줄 친 부분의 쓰임이 보기 와 같은 것을 고르세요.

보기

I know the singing girl.

① Do you like traveling by train?

② Look at the dancing girl on the stage.

③ The man was scared of sleeping alone.

④ Taking a lot of milk is good for your health.

⑤ I enjoy watching English movies.

✖ 보기 와 같이 두 문장을 한 문장으로 고쳐 쓰세요. (6~8)

보기

The woman is my mother.
She is standing at the bus stop.
→ The woman standing at the bus stop is my mother.

6 We know the man. He is reading a newspaper.
→ We know the man ______________________.

7 He bought a picture. It was painted by a famous artist.
→ He bought a picture ______________________.

8 The boy was taken to the hospital. He was injured in the traffic accident.
→ The boy ______________________ was taken to the hospital.

✖ 다음 빈칸에 들어갈 수 있는 것을 고르세요. (9~10)

9

The women look __________.

① brightly ② happily ③ interest
④ sickly ⑤ sad

10

You __________ a little tired.

① made ② saw ③ watched
④ seemed ⑤ found

Final Test

✖ 다음 (　) 안에서 알맞은 관계대명사를 고르세요. (11~12)

11 Look at the mountain (which / what / whose) top is covered with snow.

12 Science is the subject (whom / which / whose) I am most interested in.

13 빈칸에 공통으로 들어 갈 수 있는 것을 고르세요.

- There are animals ______________ live in the water.
- Look at the man ______________ wears a white shirt.

① which　② who　③ what
④ whose　⑤ that

✖ 주어진 문장을 수동태 문장으로 바꿔 쓰세요. (14~16)

14 

Peter will send this parcel tomorrow morning.

→ ______________________________ tomorrow morning.

15 

A famous architect designed this museum.

→ ______________________________ by a famous architect.

16 

Many people built the Great Wall in China more than two thousand years ago.

→ ______________________________ more than two thousand years ago.

✖ 빈칸에 들어갈 알맞은 시제를 고르세요. (17~19)

17

After Karen __________ her homework, she's going to go to bed.

① will finish ② finished ③ finishes ④ is going to finish

18

If it __________ tomorrow, I'm going to go to a movie.

① rained ② will rain ③ to rain ④ rains

19

After ancient Greek athletes won a race in the Olympics, they __________ a simple crown of olive leaves.

① received ② are going to receive ③ were receiving ④ receive

✖ 의미가 같아지도록 ( ) 안의 단어를 이용하여 알맞은 완료시제를 완성하세요. (20~21)

20

I'm looking for my key. I can't find it.

➡ ______________________________________. (lose)

21

Kevin went to Singapore. He is in Singapore.

➡ ______________________________________. (go)

Final Test

✖ too ~ to를 이용하여 한 문장으로 만들어 보세요. (22~24)

22 I am too weak. I can't move the heavy box.

➡ ______________________________.

23 She was too sleepy. She can't finish her homework.

➡ ______________________________.

24 Michael is very tired. He can't go out tonight.

➡ ______________________________.

✖ enough to를 이용하여 문장을 완성하세요. (25~27)

25 Sunny is strong enough, so she can carry the refrigerator.

➡ ______________________________.

26 I had enough time, so I watched a movie last week.

➡ ______________________________.

27 Do you have enough money? You can buy a new car.

➡ ______________________________?

✖ 주어진 단어를 이용하여 빈칸을 능동태와 수동태 문장으로 완성하세요. (28~31)

28

The fire ______________________________.

The house ______________________________. (destroyed)

29 

The students ______________________.

A summer trip ______________________. (organized)

30 

My mom ______________________ last night.

Dinner ______________________ last night. (cooked)

31 

George Lucas ______________________.

"Star Wars" ______________________. (directed)

✖ 주어진 단어를 이용하여 알맞은 과거 또는 현재완료 시제를 쓰세요. (32~34)

32 Linda and I are old friends. I ______________ (know) her since I ________ (be) a freshman in middle school.

33 Bob ______________ (have) a lot of problems since he ________ (come) to this city.

34 My wife and I have ______________ (move) three times since we ________ (get) married.

Final Test Score : (   ) of 40

✖ 다음 빈칸에 for와 since 중 알맞은 것을 써 넣으세요. (35~38)

35 I haven't seen my puppy ________ 6 months. I haven't seen my cat __________ April.

36 The world has enjoyed Beethoven's music ________ nearly 200 years.

37 He's had a bad leg __________ he was in the war.

38 Ron has worked for the company __________ 1999.

39 주어진 문장을 보기 와 같이 두 문장으로 나누어 써 보세요.

> 보기
>
> The waiter who served us dinner was rude.
>
> ➜ The waiter was rude.
>
> ➜ He served us dinner.

I wrote a letter to the woman who I met at the meeting.

➜ ____.

➜ ____.

40 주어진 두 개의 문장을 보기 와 같이 관계대명사를 이용하여 한 문장으로 다시 쓰세요.

> 보기
>
> There are many buildings.
>
> They were built two hundred years ago.
>
> ➜ There are many buildings which(that) were built two hundred years ago.

The pianist is internationally famous.

The pianist played at the concert last night.

➜ ____.

정답 및 해설

정답 및 해설

unit 01 현재완료

Target Words & Review Words
p.11, 20

- lose ⓥ 잃다
- wine ⓝ 와인[포도주]
- prepare ⓥ 준비하다
- yet ⓐⓓ (부정문에) 아직
- go to bed 자러 가다
- leg ⓝ 다리
- taste ⓥ 맛보다
- movie theater 극장
- Egypt ⓝ 이집트
- break ⓥ 깨다, 부수다
- windsurfing ⓝ 윈드 서핑
- complete ⓥ 마치다, 끝내다
- museum ⓝ 박물관
- zoo ⓝ 동물원
- wallet ⓝ 지갑
- wash a car 세차하다
- horse ⓝ 말
- already ⓐⓓ 이미, 벌써
- snake ⓝ 뱀
- ride ⓥ (말을) 타다
- take a shower 샤워하다
- travel ⓥ 여행하다

Mini Test
p.14

02 have / -ed(pp) / has
03 have(has)
04 not / never

Exercise 1
p.15

1 (1) tried (2) lost (3) lived (4) been
(5) worked (6) told (7) heard (8) studied
(9) slept (10) visited (11) seen (12) known
(13) done (14) eaten
2 (1) have lived (2) have seen (3) has finished
(4) has gone (5) has lost (6) have bought
(7) have heard

Exercise 2
p.16

1 (1) Has he washed his car?
(2) Have you been to the zoo?
(3) Have they seen the movie before?
(4) Has Tom lived in Seoul?
(5) Has Kelly been to the movie theater?
2 (1) I have not prepared for the party.
(2) I have never ridden a horse.
(3) She hasn't finished breakfast yet.

Exercise 3
p.17

1 (1) Has she lost her wallet? / she has / she hasn't
(2) I have never forgotten her name.
(3) Have you / been to Egypt / I have / I haven't
(4) Linda hasn't cleaned her room yet.
(5) Ron hasn't been to Thailand. / Has Ron been to Thailand?
2 (1) I have left my cellphone in the subway.
(2) Maria has not arrived at the City Hall yet.
(3) Linda has not finished taking a shower yet.

Jump up!
p.18

1 (1) has washed his car
(2) have gone to bed
(3) has stopped raining
(4) has broken the window
(5) has taken a shower

1 (1) 그는 그의 차를 세차했다.
➡ 세차를 다 하고 마친 상황이다. 따라서 완료시제인 have washed를 써야 한다. 하지만 주어가 3인칭 단수인 He이므로 has를 써서 has washed his car로 문장을 완성한다.
(2) 그들은 자러 갔다.
➡ 주어가 복수이므로 have를 써서 have gone to bed로 문장을 완성한다. go to bed는 '자러 가다'의 뜻이다.
(3) 비가 멈췄다.

➡ stop은 [단모음+단자음]이므로 마지막 자음 p를 한 번 더 써서 has stopped raining으로 문장을 완성한다.

(4) 누군가 창문을 깨뜨렸다.

➡ Somebody는 3인칭 단수이다. 따라서 has broken the window를 써서 문장을 완성한다.

(5) Susan은 샤워를 했다.

➡ 주어가 3인칭 단수이므로 has taken a shower로 문장을 완성한다. take a shower는 '샤워하다'의 뜻이다.

Writing Activity p.19

1 (1) Has Kevin travelled by airplane? / he hasn't / has travelled by train
(2) Has Rachel ever ridden a horse? / she has
(3) Has Robert ever tried bungee-jumping? / he hasn't / has tried windsurfing

1 (1) Kevin은 기차로 여행을 했나요? → 아니오. 그는 기차로 여행을 했습니다.
(2) Rachel은 말을 타 보았나요? → 네.
(3) Robert는 번지점프를 시도해 봤나요? → 아니오. 그는 윈드서핑을 해봤습니다.

➡ 현재완료는 have/has를 문장 맨 앞으로 보내어 의문문을 만든다. 대답 또한 have/has를 이용해서 대답한다.

Oral Test p.20

1 현재완료
2 have / -ed(pp) / has
3 have(has)
4 not / never

Unit 02 현재분사/과거분사

Target Words & Review Words p.21, 30

- ☐ cry ⓥ 울다
- ☐ shock ⓥ 충격을 주다
- ☐ recycle ⓥ 재생 이용하다
- ☐ traffic accident 교통사고
- ☐ look for 찾다, 구하다
- ☐ floor ⓝ 바닥
- ☐ disappoint ⓥ 실망시키다
- ☐ bore ⓥ 지루하게 하다
- ☐ product ⓝ 제품, 상품
- ☐ bark ⓥ 짖다
- ☐ injure ⓥ 다치게 하다
- ☐ fry ⓥ 튀기다
- ☐ vase ⓝ 꽃병, 화병
- ☐ seldom ad 거의 …않다
- ☐ twinkle ⓥ 반짝 반짝 빛나다
- ☐ be filled with ~로 가득 차다
- ☐ garage sale 차고 세일[중고 판매]
- ☐ frighten ⓥ 놀라게 하다
- ☐ wear ⓥ 입다, 쓰다
- ☐ properly ad 적절히
- ☐ novel ⓝ 소설
- ☐ freeze ⓥ 얼다
- ☐ display ⓥ 진열(전시)하다
- ☐ break ⓥ 깨다, 부수다
- ☐ hat ⓝ 모자
- ☐ machine ⓝ 기계
- ☐ bite ⓥ 물다
- ☐ noodle ⓝ 국수
- ☐ popular ⓐ 인기 있는
- ☐ dangerous ⓐ 위험한

Mini Test p.24

01 행동 / 동작
02 -ing / 뒤
03 -ed/en / 뒤

Exercise 1 p.25

1 (1) singing (2) living (3) working (4) Barking
(5) exciting (6) parked (7) written (8) cleaned
(9) interesting (10) used (11) injured (12) cooking
(13) boring (14) made (15) frozen

Exercise 2 p.26

1 (1) smiling (2) boiling (3) taking
(4) interesting (5) singing (6) reading
(7) cooking (8) wearing (9) running
(10) smiling

Exercise 3

p.27

1 (1) written (2) fried (3) written (4) called
(5) stolen (6) made (7) frozen (8) invited
(9) taken (10) painted

Jump up!

p.28

1 (1) broken vase
(2) reading a book
(3) written in easy English
2 (1) ② (2) ③

1 (1) 바닥에 저 깨진 꽃병을 보아라.
➡ 명사 vase가 직접 행동을 하는게 아니라 깨진 동작을 받은, 당하는 의미이므로 broken을 앞에 써서 표현을 한다.
(2) 책을 읽고 있는 소녀들은 내 친구들이다.
➡ 명사 뒤에서 분사가 꾸밀 경우 분사와 함께 명사를 꾸며주는 말이 더 붙을 경우 명사 뒤에서 꾸며준다. 소녀들이 책을 읽는 주인[주체]이므로 read를 reading으로 바꿔 The girls reading a book 처럼 '책을 읽는 소녀들'이란 말로 문장을 완성한다.
(3) 쉬운 영어로 쓰여진 이 책은 매우 인기가 좋다.
➡ 책이라는 명사를 꾸며주는 분사 이외에 몇 개 단어가 더 있을 경우 명사 뒤에서 꾸며준다. 책(book)은 행동을 할 수 있는 주인이 될 수 없으므로 written in easy English로 만들어 명사(this book) 뒤에서 명사를 꾸며주어야 한다.

2 (1) 자라는 아이들은 많은 음식을 먹는다.
➡ '자라는 아이들'에서 '자라다'의 grow를 growing으로 고치고, 명사 앞에 놓으면 '자라는 아이들(growing children)'로 문장이 완성된다. 명사의 행위나 동작을 꾸며주는 말이 한 단어일 때는 명사 바로 앞에서 꾸며준다.
(2) 나는 저 유리창 안에 진열된 옷을 좋아한다.
➡ 옷(dress)은 스스로 행동을 하는 주인이 될 수 없다. 따라서 displayed라는 과거분사 형태가 들어가야 한다.

Writing Activity

p.29

1 (1) built one hundred years ago
(2) twinkling in the sky
(3) crying in the park is my daughter
(4) made in Korea
2 (1) disappointing / disappointed
(2) frightening / frightened

1 (1) 이것은 교회이다. + 그것은 백년 전에 지어졌다.
→ 이것은 백년 전에 지어진 교회이다.
➡ 백년 전에 지어진 교회라는 뜻을 만들기 위해서 교회(church)라는 명사 뒤에서 꾸며주는 역할을 해주어야 한다. 특히 명사(church)는 행동을 하는 주인이 될 수 없으므로 build의 과거분사인 built를 써서 built one hundred years ago로 영작을 해야 한다.
(2) 별들을 보아라. + 그들은 하늘에서 반짝이고 있다. → 하늘에서 반짝이고 있는 별들을 보아라.
➡ '반짝 반짝 빛나다'의 뜻인 twinkle은 명사 stars를 꾸며주는 역할을 해야 한다. 별들이 반짝이고 있는 행동의 주인이 될 수 있으므로 twinkling in the sky를 써서 명사 뒤에서 명사를 꾸며주는 역할을 해야 한다.
(3) 그 소녀는 내 딸이다. + 그녀는 공원에서 울고 있다. → 공원에서 울고 있는 그 소녀가 내 딸이다.
➡ 공원에서 (in the park) 울고 있는 (crying) 소녀 (the girl)란 표현으로 영작을 해야 한다. 하지만 in the park와 함께 명사를 꾸며주어야 하므로 명사 뒤에서 꾸며주는 역할을 해야 한다. 명사(girl)가 울고 있는 행동의 주인이므로 현재분사인 crying으로 만들어 영작한다.
(4) 이것은 디지털 카메라이다. + 그것은 한국에서 만들어졌다. → 이것은 한국에서 만들어진 디지

털 카메라이다.

➡ 한국에서(in Korea) 만들어진(made) 카메라(camera)가 되어야 한다. 하지만 꾸며주는 말이 분사 말고 몇 개 더 있을 경우 명사 뒤에서 꾸며주어야 한다. 따라서 a digital camera made in Korea 라고 영작해야 한다.

2 (1) 그 영화는 너를 실망시킨다.
→ 그 영화는 실망스럽다. [실망시켰다]
→ 너는 실망했다. [실망을 받았다]
(2) 그 이상한 여자는 아이들을 무섭게 했다.
→ 그 이상한 여자는 무섭게 했다. [무서움을 주었다]
→ 아이들은 무서워 했다. [무서움을 받았다]

➡ 감정을 나타내는 동사에 –ing를 붙이거나 –ed를 붙여 분사를 만들 경우 감정을 주는 주체는 언제나 –ing를 쓰고, 감정을 받는 대상은 –ed를 써서 영작해야 한다.

Oral Test p. 30

1 행동/동작
2 현재분사 / 과거분사
3 –ing / 뒤
4 –ed/en

unit 03 부사 역할의 부정사

Target Words & Review Words p. 34, 40

□ bookstore ⓝ 서점	□ wear ⓥ 입다, 쓰다, 신다
□ present ⓝ 선물	□ full ⓐ 가득한
□ save ⓥ 저축하다, 모으다	□ bakery ⓝ 제과점
□ education ⓝ 교육	□ discussion ⓝ 토론, 논의
□ pocket ⓝ 호주머니	□ school record 학교 성적
□ pleased ⓐ 기뻐하는	□ recycle ⓥ 재생 이용하다
□ environment ⓝ 환경	□ sportswear ⓝ 운동복
□ airport ⓝ 공항	□ glad ⓐ 기쁜
□ news ⓝ 뉴스, 소식	□ job ⓝ 직업
□ research ⓝ 연구, 조사	□ bare ⓐ 벌거벗은, 맨손의
□ invite ⓥ 초대하다	□ protect ⓥ 막다, 보호하다
□ put on 입다	□ post office 우체국

□ turn on (전기, TV 등을) 켜다
□ native ⓐ (그 고장) 태생인, 원주민의
□ concert ⓝ 콘서트, 음악회, 공연
□ mail ⓥ 우송하다, 우편으로 부치다

Mini Test p. 34

02 ~하기 위하여
03 감정/느낌
04 앞

Exercise 1 p. 35

1 (1) to buy (2) to know (3) to learn (4) to help
(5) to watch (6) to buy
2 (1) for some fruit (2) for a letter
(3) for our friends (4) for him

Exercise 2 p. 36

1 (1) to (2) to (3) to (4) to (5) for (6) for
(7) to (8) to (9) for (10) for
2 (1) too (2) too (3) enough (4) enough (5) too
(6) enough

Exercise 3
p.37

1 (1) I am too weak to carry this big schoolbag.
(2) My cat is too young to catch a mouse.
(3) Tommy is too sleepy to study.
(4) She was too sad to talk to anyone.

Jump up!
p.38

1 (1) high enough to go
(2) smart enough to solve
(3) strong enough to kill
2 (1) She was surprised to get a letter.
(2) Are you happy to go to the party?
(3) I was pleased to eat such delicious food.
(4) My mom was shocked to hear the news.

1 (1) ➡ '~할 정도로'의 뜻은 [enough to 부정사]를 사용한다. 형용사 high는 enough 앞에 써야 한다. 따라서 high enough to go로 문장을 완성한다.
(2) ➡ 마찬가지로 형용사 smart는 enough 앞에 써서 smart enough to solve로 문장을 완성한다.
(3) ➡ 형용사 strong을 enough 앞에 써서 strong enough to kill로 쓴다. to 뒤에는 동사원형을 쓴다.

2 (1) 그녀는 놀랐었다. + 그녀는 편지를 받았다.
→ 그녀는 편지를 받아서 놀랐었다.
➡ 사람의 감정을 나타내는 분사 surprised 뒤에 부정사를 써서 우리말 '~해서(원인)'의 뜻이 된다. 따라서 과거동사 got을 to get으로 바꿔 감정 형용사 surprised 뒤에 붙여 쓴다.
(2) 행복하니? + 너는 파티에 갈거다.
→ 너는 파티에 가게 되서 행복하니?
➡ 감정 형용사 happy 뒤에 to 부정사를 쓴다. 따라서 will go를 to go로 고쳐 happy 뒤에 붙여 쓴다.
(3) 나는 기뻤다. + 나는 그런 맛있는 음식을 먹었다. → 나는 그러한 맛있는 음식을 먹어서 기뻤다.
➡ pleased는 기쁨을 나타내는 감정 형용사이다. 따라서 ate를 to eat으로 고쳐 감정 형용사 뒤에 붙여 쓴다.
(4) 나의 엄마는 충격을 받았다. 그녀는 그 소식을 들었다. → 나의 엄마는 그 소식을 듣고 충격을 받았다.
➡ 사람의 감정을 나타내는 shocked 뒤에 to hear the news를 쓴다.

Writing Activity
p.39

1 (1) She called Justin to invite him to her party.
(2) He is going to Pizza Hut to have dinner.
(3) They recycle old newspapers and books to protect the environment.
(4) He put on his sportswear to go jogging.
(5) He went to the post office to mail a letter.

1 (1) 왜 Christina는 어제 Justin에게 전화를 했나요?
그녀는 Justin을 그녀의 파티에 초대 하기위해 전화를 했다.
➡ 동사의 구체적인 목적을 표현하기 위해 to 부정사를 쓴다. 따라서 to invite him to her party를 써서 문장을 완성한다.
(2) 왜 Peter는 오늘밤 피자헛에 가려고 하나요?
그는 저녁 식사를 하기 위해서 피자헛에 갈 겁니다.
➡ '저녁식사를 하기 위하여'는 to have dinner로 쓴다. 이 표현을 He is going to Pizza Hut 뒤에 붙여 [be going to + 장소]의 구체적인 목적을 말해줄 수 있다.
(3) 왜 그들은 오래된 신문지와 책들을 재활용하나요?
그들은 환경을 보호하기 위하여 오래된 신문과 책들을 재활용합니다.

➡ '환경을 보호하기 위하여'의 뜻을 만들면 to protect the environment가 된다. 이 표현을 동사의 구체적인 목적을 나타내주기 위해서 They recycle old newspapers and books 뒤에 붙여 표현하면 된다.

(4) 왜 Ron은 그의 운동복을 입었나요?
그는 조깅하러 가기 위해서 운동복을 입었다.

➡ '조깅하러 하기 위하여'의 뜻을 만들면 to go jogging이 된다. 여기서 [go+-ing]는 '~하러 가다'의 표현이다. 이 표현을 동사의 구체적인 목적을 나타내기 위하여 Ron put on his sportswear 뒤에 붙여 써주면 된다.

(5) 왜 Tom은 우체국에 갔나요?
그는 편지를 부치기 위하여 우체국에 갔다.

➡ '편지를 부치기 위하여'의 뜻을 만들면 to mail a letter가 된다. 이 표현을 동사 went to the post office 뒤에 두어서 동사의 구체적인 목적을 나타내주면 된다.

Oral Test p. 40

1 부사적
2 ~하기 위하여
3 원인
4 형용사 / 형용사 / 앞

unit 04 현재완료 계속

Target Words & Review Words p. 41, 50

- still ad 여전히, 아직도
- uncle ⓝ 삼촌
- each other 서로 서로
- biology ⓝ 생물학
- stamp ⓝ 우표
- history ⓝ 역사
- company ⓝ 회사
- phone bill 전화 요금
- abroad ad 해외에[로]
- meal ⓝ 식사
- programmer ⓝ 프로그래머
- collect ⓥ 모으다, 수집하다
- freshman ⓝ 신입생, 1학년생
- everywhere ad 도처에, 모든 곳에
- make friends 친구를 사귀다
- elementary ⓐ 초등학교의
- teach ⓥ 가르치다
- rise ⓥ (값이) 오르다
- improve ⓥ 향상시키다
- movie star 영화배우
- accident ⓝ 사고
- marry ⓥ ~와 결혼하다
- Thailand ⓝ 태국
- begin ⓥ 시작하다

Mini Test p. 44

02 for
03 since / since / 과거
04 for / since

Exercise 1 p. 45

1 (1) since (2) for (3) for (4) since (5) since
(6) for (7) since (8) for (9) for (10) since
(11) for (12) for (13) since (14) since (15) for

Exercise 2 p. 46

1 (1) have known / ten years
(2) has worked / since (3) have met / was
(4) has had / came (5) have known / were
(6) has risen / bought
2 (1) have you known (2) have you studied
(3) has your sister worked (4) have you been

Exercise 3 p. 47

1 (1) have lived / since (2) has taught / for
(3) has travelled / since (4) has improved / since
2 (1) has collected stamps for two years
(2) have worked for the company since 1995
(3) has rained (everywhere) since last night

Jump up! p. 48

1 ④
2 (1) has lived / for (2) have been / since
(3) has read / since (4) has lived / for
(5) have been / since (6) has talked / for

1 ➡ 현재완료 계속은 그 기간을 나타내주는 for나 since와 함께 쓰일 때 계속을 나타낸다. 따라서 ④번이 현재완료 계속이다.

2 (1) Lisa는 5개월 전에 시애틀에서 살기 시작했다. 그녀는 여전히 그곳에서 살고 있다. → Lisa는 5개월동안 시애틀에서 살고 있다.
➡ 5개월이라는 기간의 표현이 있고 주어가 3인칭 단수이므로 has lived를 쓰고 전치사 for를 기간 앞에 쓴다. ago는 과거를 정확히 표현하므로 ago를 함께 써서는 안 된다.
(2) 나는 Karen을 2006년에 처음 만났다. Karen과 나는 여전히 좋은 친구사이다. → Karen과 나는 2006년 이래로 좋은 친구사이다.
➡ 과거와 현재를 연결해 주어야 하므로 완료시제 have been을 쓴다. 처음 알게 된 것이 2006년부터라는 과거의 시작점(starting point)만 있으므로 since로 연결시켜 주어야 한다.
(3) Linda는 지난 월요일에 두 권의 역사책을 읽었다. 그녀는 여전히 그 책들을 읽고 있다. → Linda는 지난 월요일 이래로 두 권의 역사책을 읽고 있다.
➡ 과거와 현재를 연결시키는 완료 시제인 has read를 쓰고 과거의 시작한 점만을 알 수 있으므로 since를 써야 한다.
(4) Sunny는 10년 전에 뉴욕에서 살았다. 그녀는 여전히 그곳에서 산다. → Sunny는 10년 동안 뉴욕에서 살고 있다.
➡ 과거와 현재를 연결해주는 시제 has lived를 쓰고 10년 동안이라는 기간이 있으므로 전치사 for를 이용해서 문장을 완성한다.
(5) 그들은 2007년에 결혼했다. 그들은 여전히 결혼한 상태이다. → 그들은 2007년 이래로 결혼한 상태이다.
➡ 과거와 현재를 연결해주는 시제 have been married를 쓰고 2007년부터라는 과거의 시작점의 표현이 있으므로 since를 이용해서 문장을 완성한다.
(6) Peter는 3시간 전에 전화 통화를 시작했다. 그는 여전히 전화 통화를 하고 있다. → Peter는 3시간 동안 전화 통화를 하고 있다.
➡ 과거와 현재를 연결하는 has talked를 쓰고 3시간 동안이라는 기간이 있으므로 for를 써서 문장을 완성한다.

Writing Activity p. 49

1 (1) How long have you had your driving licence? / Have / had / haven't
(2) How long have you been in Seoul? / Have / made / have made
(3) How long have you studied English? / haven't spoken / have watched
(4) How long have you worked here? / have been / have worked / since

1 (1) A: 당신은 얼마나 오래 운전면허증을 소지하고 계셨나요?
B: 2년 동안 소지하고 있어요.
A: 사고를 낸 적이 있나요?
B: 아니오, 없습니다.
(2) A: 당신은 얼마나 오랫동안 서울에 있었나요?
B: 2006년부터 있었어요.
A: 친구들 좀 사귀었나요?

B: 네, 많은 친구들을 사귀었어요, 그런데 한국어는 늘지가 않았어요.

(3) A: 당신은 얼마나 오랫동안 영어공부를 했나요?

B: 6년 동안 했어요. 그런데 영어를 안한지 오래됐어요.

A: 나도 마찬가지예요. 나는 미국인들과 대화를 하지는 않지만 수년 동안 영어로 된 영화는 보고있어요.

(4) A: 당신은 여기서 얼마나 오랫동안 일했나요?

B: 5월부터 일했어요. 그러나 나는 10년 동안 컴퓨터 프로그래머 일을 했어요.

A: 다른 회사에서 일을 해본 적 있나요?

B: 네, 1999년 이래로 3곳의 회사에서 일을 했어요.

➡ How long은 기간을 물어보는 의문사로 현재완료와 함께 쓴다. have동사의 완료시제는 have had를 쓴다. 기간을 물어보는 의문문이므로 현재완료를 이용해 대답한다. 완료시제로 물어보는 의문문에 짧게 대답할 때는 긍정으로 대답할 때는 [Yes, S+have/has.], 부정은 [No, S+haven't /hasn't.]를 쓴다.

Oral Test

p. 50

1 for 2 since / since / 과거 3 for / since

Progress Test 1

p. 52~54

1 have lived 2 have seen 3 has finished
4 has gone 5 sleeping 6 used 7 watching
8 I am too weak to carry this big box.
9 We are very hungry enough to eat anything.
10 ① 11 ② 12 ① 13 written 14 dancing
15 made 16 wearing
17 How long have you worked for the company?
18 How long have you studied English?
19 We've lived in Seattle since 2005.
20 Lisa has taught English for five months.

unit 05 2, 4, 5형식 동사

Target Words & Review Words

p. 55, 64

- ☐ look ⓥ ~처럼 보이다
- ☐ sound ⓥ ~처럼 들리다
- ☐ serious ⓐ 심각한
- ☐ green tea 녹차
- ☐ dead ⓐ 죽은
- ☐ thirsty ⓐ 목마른
- ☐ taste ⓥ ~처럼 맛이 나다
- ☐ allow ⓥ 허락하다
- ☐ send ⓥ 보내다, 부치다
- ☐ advise ⓥ 충고하다
- ☐ partner ⓝ 동료, 상대방
- ☐ upset ⓐ 기분이 상한, 화가 난
- ☐ feel ⓥ ~처럼 느끼다
- ☐ terrible ⓐ 지독한
- ☐ voice ⓝ 목소리, 음성
- ☐ message ⓝ 메시지, 용건
- ☐ mental hospital 정신 병원
- ☐ seem ⓥ ~처럼 보이다
- ☐ take a picture 사진을 찍다
- ☐ rough ⓐ 거칠거칠한
- ☐ stand up 일어서다
- ☐ cheer up 힘내다

Mini Test

p. 58

01 형용사 / 형용사
02 전치사 / to / for
03 명사 / 형용사 / to 부정사

Exercise 1

p. 59

1 (1) terrible (2) happy (3) bad (4) wise
(5) looks / strong (6) taste / sweet (7) serious
(8) feels / rough
2 (1) sounds (2) smells (3) feel (4) looked
(5) tastes

Exercise 2

p. 60

1 (1) us English (2) her my picture
(3) me an e-mail (4) us some cookies
(5) him chocolates (6) my son a bike
(7) you a gift (8) it to her
2 (1) for (2) to (3) to (4) to (5) to (6) for

Exercise 3

p. 61

1 (1) to stand (2) to be (3) dead (4) to go
(5) a big star (6) to spend (7) me (8) difficult

2 (1) to take (2) to help (3) to come (4) to marry
(5) to cheer (6) to go (7) to exercise

Jump up! p. 62

1 (1) Karen some flowers / some flowers to Karen
(2) me a sweater / a sweater for me
2 (1) looks hungry (2) looks thirsty
(3) look angry (4) look happy

1 (1) Tom은 Karen에게 약간의 꽃을 주었다.
➡ 4형식 동사는 [사람 (~에게)+사물(…을/를)]을 위해 목적어 두 개를 필요로 한다. 4형식을 3형식으로 고칠 때 사물을 먼저 쓰고 사람을 뒤에 쓸 경우 사람명사 앞에 전치사를 써주어야 한다. give는 전치사 to를 쓰는 동사이다.
(2) 내 친구는 나에게 스웨터를 만들어 주었다.
➡ made me a sweater를 써서 동사 뒤에 사람, 그리고 연이어 사물명사를 쓴다. make 동사는 3형식으로 만들 경우 사람명사 앞에 전치사 for를 쓴다.

2 (1) 그녀는 배고픈 것처럼 보인다.
➡ 주어가 3인칭 단수 이므로 looks를 쓰고 2형식 동사 look 뒤에는 형용사만 쓸 수 있다.
(2) 그녀는 목마른 것처럼 보인다.
➡ 마찬가지로 look 뒤에 thirsty라는 형용사만을 보어로 쓴다.
(3) 그들은 화난 것처럼 보인다.
➡ 우리말에 '화나게 보인다'로 해석할 경우 angry가 아닌 부사 angrily를 쓸 것 같지만 절대 써서는 안 된다. 언제나 주어의 상태를 설명하는 것은 형용사만이 가능하다. 따라서 angry를 보어로 써야 한다.
(4) 그들은 행복한 것처럼 보인다.
➡ '행복하게 보인다'로 해석하면 부사 happily를 쓸 것처럼 착각을 할 수 있다. 언제나 주어의 상태를 설명하는 것은 happy인 형용사만이 가능하다.

Writing Activity p. 63

1 (1) told me to stop
(2) advised Peter to lose ten kilograms
(3) asked her partner to help
(4) asked Nancy to have a cup of coffee

1 (1) 그 여성은 "당신은 여기에서 멈춰야 합니다"라고 말했다.
→ 그 여성은 우리에게 멈추라고 말했다. (5형식 문장)
➡ 5형식은 [목적어+목적격 보어]를 이용해 문장을 만든다. 특히 목적어의 동작이나 행위가 필요할 경우 목적격 보어 자리에 'to 부정사'를 써야 한다. 따라서 told me to stop으로 영작해 주면 된다.
(2) 그 의사는 "Peter, 당신은 10kg 정도 살을 빼야 합니다"라고 말했다.
→ 그 의사는 Peter에게 10kg 정도 살을 빼라고 충고했다. (5형식 문장)
➡ advice라는 5형식 동사를 이용하여 문장을 완성한다. 목적어로 Peter를 쓰고 목적격 보어는 to 부정사를 써야 하므로 to lose ten kilograms를 써서 문장을 완성한다.
(3) Lisa는 그의 파트너에게 "이 문제를 푸는 것 좀 도와줄래?"라고 말했다.
→ Lisa는 그의 파트너에게 이 문제를 푸는 것을 도와달라고 요청했다. (5형식 문장)
➡ asked 뒤에 목적어(her partner)와 목적격 보어(to help her with that question)를 써서 문장을 완성한다.
(4) Sunny는 Nancy에게 "수업 후에 나랑 같이 커피 한 잔 할래?"라고 말했다.
→ Sunny는 Nancy에게 수업 후에 커피 한 잔 하자고 요청했다. (5형식 문장)
➡ 동사 asked 뒤에 목적어(Nancy)와 목적격 보어

(to have a cup of coffee)를 써서 문장을 완성한다.

Oral Test p. 64

1 형용사
2 전치사 / to / for
3 명사 / 형용사 / to 부정사

unit 06 동명사

Target Words & Review Words p. 65, 74

- necessary ⓐ 필요한
- ski ⓥ 스키를 타다
- sell ⓥ ~을 팔다
- midnight ⓝ (한)밤중
- kite ⓝ 연
- beach ⓝ 해변가
- work out 운동하다
- health ⓝ 건강
- rest ⓝ 휴식
- language ⓝ 언어
- stand ⓥ 참다, 견디다
- course ⓝ 과목, 강좌
- tidy ⓥ 정돈하다
- be afraid of ~을 무서워 하다
- over and over again 되풀이해서
- be proud of ~를 자랑스러워 하다
- on one's way home 집에 가는 도중에
- be interested in ~에 관심[흥미]이 있다
- rock ⓝ 바위, 암벽
- school days 학창 시절
- foreign ⓐ 외국의
- insist ⓥ 주장하다
- continue ⓥ 계속되다
- prepare ⓥ 준비하다
- climb ⓥ (~을) 기어오르다
- regret ⓥ 후회하다
- dark ⓐ 어두운
- neighbor ⓝ 이웃(사람)
- quit ⓥ ~을 그만두다
- especially ⓐⓓ 특히

Mini Test p. 68

01 명사
02 1 주어 2 목적어 3 보어 4 동명사
04 not

Exercise 1 p. 69

1 (1) 주어 (2) 목적어 (3) 목적어 (4) 보어
(5) 보어 (6) 목적어 (7) 주어 (8) 보어 (9) 주어
(10) 목적어
2 (1) being (2) coming (3) going (4) opening
(5) watching (6) flying

Exercise 2 p. 70

1 (1) The boy began singing.
(2) Ted hates doing his homework.
(3) She can't stand waiting in a long line.
(4) Mary likes sitting in front of the television.
(5) They started fighting.
(6) Does she love flying kites?
(7) His neighbor continued talking about Sunny's car.
2 (1) 왜 너는 서울에서 사는 것을 싫어하니?
(2) 나의 엄마의 취미는 수영하는 것이다.

Exercise 3 p. 71

1 (1) listening (2) raining (3) smoking
(4) closing (5) answering (6) watching
2 (1) kept looking (2) mind closing
(3) enjoy skiing

Jump up! p. 72

1 (1) ① (2) ② (3) ① (4) ① (5) ② (6) ①
(7) ① (8) ②

1 (1) 나는 지난여름 가족과 함께 바닷가에 있었던 것을 즐겼다.
➡ enjoy 동사 뒤에 목적어로 동명사를 받는다. 동명사와 부정사 둘 다 동작이나 행위를 표현해 주지만, 동명사는 이미 경험했거나 그 행위를 해봤던[했던] 것에 초점을 두고 있다. 따라서 동명사 행태인 being을 쓰는 것이 적절하다.
(2) 나는 다른 직업을 찾기로 결정했다.
➡ decide 동사 뒤에는 부정사를 목적어로 받는다.

다른 직업을 찾기로 결정한 것이지 아직 찾은 것은 아니기 때문에 행위나 행동을 앞으로 해야 할 것에는 부정사를 쓰는 것이 보통이다.

(3) Justin, 집에 돌아가는 길에 이 편지를 부쳐줄 수 있나요?

➡ mind 뒤에는 목적어로 동명사를 쓴다.

(4) 마침내, 나는 기말시험 준비를 끝냈다.

➡ finish 뒤에는 목적어로 동명사를 쓴다.

(5) 이 과목을 통과 할 것으로 기대 하나요? 만약 그렇다면, 당신은 더 열심히 공부해야 합니다.

➡ expect 뒤에는 부정사를 목적어로 쓴다.

(6) 오늘밤에 모이자. 나는 새로운 개업에 대해 얘기하고 싶다.

➡ 전치사 about 뒤에는 동명사를 쓴다.

(7) 왜 너는 나에게 똑같은 질문을 몇 번이고 되풀이해서 물어보는 거니?

➡ keep 뒤에 동명사를 쓴다. [keep+-ing]는 keep 동사의 성질 때문에 '계속해서 ~하다'의 의미가 된다.

(8) 나에게 책과 글을 써 보내주신 것에 대해 감사합니다. 나는 특히 해리포터 시리즈를 정말 즐겁게 읽었습니다.

➡ 전치사 for 뒤에는 동명사를 써야 한다. 그리고 enjoy 뒤에는 목적어로 동명사만을 받는다.

Writing Activity p. 73

1 (1) doesn't mind tidying her room
(2) is interested in getting a job at a hotel
(3) hates washing her feet
(4) enjoys taking pictures
(5) can't stand waking up early

1 (1) Nancy는 그녀의 방을 정돈하는 것에 신경 쓰지 않는다.

➡ mind 뒤에 동명사를 목적어로 사용해 doesn't mind tidying her room으로 문장을 완성한다.

(2) Nancy는 호텔에서 일하는 것에 관심을 가지고 있다.

➡ be interested in는 '~에 흥미[관심]가 있다'의 표현으로 전치사 in이 있기 때문에 동명사인 getting을 쓴다.

(3) Nancy는 그녀의 발을 씻는 것을 싫어한다.

➡ hate 뒤에 동명사를 써서 washing her feet으로 영작한다.

(4) Nancy는 사진 찍는 것을 즐긴다.

➡ enjoy 뒤에는 동명사(taking)가 온다.

(5) Nancy는 일찍 일어나는 것을 견디지 못한다.

➡ [stand+-ing]는 '~하는 것을 참다, 견디다'의 뜻이 있다. 따라서 can't stand 뒤에 wake를 waking으로 고쳐 영작한다.

Oral Test p. 74

1 명사
2 주어
3 목적어
4 보어
5 동명사
6 동명사
7 not

Unit 07 수동태

Target Words & Review Words p. 75, 84

□ paint ⓥ (그림을) 그리다	□ mirror ⓝ 거울
□ temple ⓝ 사원	□ rice ⓝ 쌀
□ hire ⓥ 고용하다	□ careless ⓐ 부주의한
□ package ⓝ 소포	□ wallet ⓝ 지갑
□ deliver ⓥ 배달하다	□ invent ⓥ 발명하다
□ tax ⓝ 세금	□ drug ⓝ 약, 약품
□ serve ⓥ (음식물을) 제공하다	□ picture ⓝ 그림, 사진
□ invite ⓥ 초대하다	□ destroy ⓥ 파괴하다
□ grow ⓥ 재배하다	□ film ⓝ 영화
□ accident ⓝ 사고	□ neighbor ⓝ 이웃(사람)
□ fix ⓥ 고치다	□ light bulb 백열 전구
□ government ⓝ 정부	□ drink ⓝ 음료, 마실 것
□ open ⓥ (가게 등을) 열다	
□ ingredient ⓝ 성분, 요소, 원료	

Mini Test p. 78

01 be / 과거분사
03 not / be

Exercise 1 p. 79

1 (1) broke / broken (2) asked / asked
(3) bought / bought (4) did / done
(5) knew / known (6) took / taken
(7) wrote / written (8) made / made
(9) built / built (10) spoke / spoken
(11) stole / stolen (12) told / told (13) drew / drawn
(14) painted / painted (15) lost / lost
(16) taught / taught (17) gave / given
(18) grew / grown

Exercise 2 p. 80

1 (1) was broken (2) loves (3) is read
(4) were invited (5) causes (6) helps
(7) are helped
2 (1) The letter wasn't written by Justin.
(2) This house wasn't built 100 years ago.
(3) The package wasn't mailed by Peter.
(4) Susan wasn't hired by that company.
(5) The children weren't found by a neighbor last night.

Exercise 3 p. 81

1 (1) Your life is changed by books.
(2) The work was finished by Karen.
(3) The glasses were broken by Lucy.
(4) The accident was seen by many people.
(5) These pictures were taken by Christina.
2 (1) Is this e-mail written by her? / it is
(2) Was the work done by him? / it wasn't
(3) Was your wallet stolen on the subway? / it was
(4) Were these bikes fixed by your dad? / they weren't

Jump up! p. 82

1 (1) Our mail is delivered
(2) The cake was eaten yesterday
2 (1) invented the light bulb / was invented by Thomas Edison
(2) collects taxes / are collected by the government
(3) wrote the book *War and Peace* / was written by Leo Tolstoy

1 (1) 우리의 우편물은 Mr. Kevin에 의해서 배달된다.
➡ 수동태 문장은 행위의 대상인 사물 등을 문장 앞의 주어 자리에 두고 동사를 [be+과거분사] 형태로 만들어 사용한다. 따라서 Our mail is delivered를 써야 한다. be 동사는 대상 주어의 단수/복수 여부에 따라서 is/are을 구별해서 써야 한다.
(2) 그 케이크는 그들에 의해서 어제 먹혀졌다. (그들이 어제 케이크를 먹었다.)

➡ the cake를 주어로 쓰고 eat을 was eaten으로 쓴다.

2 (1) Thomas Edison이 백열전구를 발명했다.
백열전구는 Thomas Edison에 의해서 발명되었다.
➡ 능동태는 [invented+목적어]를 쓰고, 수동태는 [목적어+was invented by]로 쓴다.

(2) 정부는 세금을 모은다.
세금은 정부에 의해서 모아진다.
➡ 능동태는 [collects+목적어]를 쓰고, 수동태는 [목적어+are collected by]를 쓴다. 이때 주어(Taxes)는 복수이므로 be동사 are을 쓴다.

(3) Leo Tolstoy는 전쟁과 평화라는 책을 썼다.
전쟁과 평화라는 책은 Leo Tolstoy에 의해서 쓰여졌다.
➡ 능동태는 [wrote+목적어]를 쓰고, 수동태는 [목적어+was written by]로 쓴다. 주어가 3인칭 단수인 The book이므로 be동사는 was를 써야 한다.

Writing Activity

p. 83

1 (1) Coca-Cola is drunk all over the world.
(2) The drink was invented in 1886 by John Pemberton.
(3) It was sold as a drug.
(4) The ingredients of Coca-Cola are not known.
(5) The first McDonald's restaurant was opened by the McDonald brothers in California in 1949.
(6) Only three things were served by the restaurant: hamburgers, French fries, and milkshakes.
(7) More than 40 million hamburgers are eaten every day (by people).

1 (1) 코카콜라는 전 세계에서 마신다.
➡ 목적어인 Coca-Cola를 주어에 두고 동사를 is drunk으로 쓴다.

(2) 그 음료는 1886년 John Pemberton에 의해서 발명되었다.
➡ 목적어인 the drink를 주어에 쓰고 동사를 was invented로 바꿔 영작한다.

(3) 그것은 약품으로 판매되었다.
➡ 목적어 it을 주어로 두고 동사를 was sold를 써서 문장을 완성한다.

(4) 코카콜라의 성분은 알려지지 않았다.
➡ 목적어 the ingredients를 주어자리에 쓰고 동사를 are not known으로 영작한다.

(5) 첫 번째 맥도날드의 가게는 1949년 캘리포니아에서 맥도날드 형제에 의해서 시작되었다.
➡ 목적어 The first McDonald's restaurant를 주어로 쓰고 동사 opened를 was opened로 바꿔 영작한다.

(6) 그 가게에서는 햄버거, 프렌치프라이, 밀크쉐이크 단 3개의 음식만 제공되었다.
➡ 목적어 only three things를 주어에 쓰고 동사 served를 were served로 고쳐 영작한다.

(7) 4천만 개 이상의 햄버거가 매일 소비된다.[먹혀진다.]
➡ 목적어 more than 40 million hamburgers를 주어로 쓰고 동사 eat을 are eaten으로 바꿔 영작한다. people은 일반인 주어이므로 by people로 써도 되고 생략해도 된다.

Oral Test

p. 84

1 be+과거분사
2 not
3 be동사 / 대명사 / be동사

unit 08 과거와 현재완료

Target Words & Review Words

p. 85, 94

- headache ⓝ 두통
- ghost ⓝ 귀신, 유령
- history ⓝ 역사
- break out 발생(돌발)하다
- volleyball ⓝ 배구
- cast ⓝ 깁스, 붕대
- visit ⓥ 방문하다
- hiking ⓝ 도보 여행
- news ⓝ 뉴스, 소식
- delicious ⓐ 맛있는
- Korean War 한국 전쟁
- photographer ⓝ 사진가
- look for ~을 찾다, 구하다
- fix ⓥ 고치다
- strange ⓐ 이상한, 낯선
- anchor ⓝ 앵커[뉴스 진행자]
- waterski ⓥ 수상스키를 타다
- teenager ⓝ 10대의 소년, 소녀

Mini Test

p. 88

01 과거 / 현재
02 현재

Exercise 1

p. 89

1 (1) finished (2) have finished (3) see (4) seen
(5) visited (6) has visited (7) saw (8) have seen

2 (1) have known (2) read (3) eaten (4) broke
(5) lived (6) have lived

Exercise 2

p. 90

1 (1) has been (2) have played (3) has read
(4) has broken (5) has lost
(6) has bought / bought

Exercise 3

p. 91

1 (1) saw / have not seen
(2) Have / fixed
(3) did / do / stayed
(4) Have / finished / finished
(5) Have / been / went
(6) Have / ever played / played
(7) did / go / went
(8) have just finished

Jump up!

p. 92

1 ③
2 ②
3 ②

1 ➡ when은 특정한 과거의 시점을 정확하게 짚어서 말하는 표현이므로 빈칸에는 과거 시제를 써야 한다. 따라서 ③번이 알맞다.

2 ➡ 현재완료를 써서 의문문을 만들고 긍정의 대답이 필요하다. 대답을 할 때는 yesterday라는 과거의 시점이 언급되었으므로, 과거형동사를 써서 대답한다. 따라서 ②번이 정답이다. 현재완료 의문문과 함께 쓰이는 yet은 '벌써'라는 의미를 가진다.

3 ➡ ②번을 제외한 나머지 표현은 모두 과거를 정확하게 표현하는 것들이다. 따라서 ②번만이 현재완료 시제와 함께 쓸 수 있다.

Writing Activity

p. 93

1 (1) Have you ever visited Egypt? / have / visited Egypt two years ago
(2) Have you ever eaten Korean food? / have / ate Korean food yesterday
(3) Has Sunny tried waterskiing? / has / tried waterskiing last month

1 (1) 너는 이집트에 가본 적이 있니? 응, 나는 2년 전에 가봤어.
➡ ever를 이용한 현재완료 경험을 물어본다. 따라서 '가본 적이 있니?'를 물어볼 때는 [Have you ever+과거분사?]로 물어본다. 현재완료 의문문에 대답은 have를 사용해서 답하고, '~년 전에'라는 과거 시제에 맞게 문장을 쓸 때는 과거시제인 visited만 써서 문장을 영작해야 한

다.

(2) 한국 음식을 먹어 본 적이 있니? 응, 나는 어제 먹어 봤어.

➡ 상대방에게 경험을 물어보는 의문문이므로 Have you ever eaten ~?으로 의문문을 만들고 대답은 have를 이용해서 대답한다. 어제 먹어 봤다는 말은 과거이므로 동사 eat의 과거인 ate만 써서 문장을 완성해야 한다.

(3) Sunny는 수상스키를 타 본 적이 있니? 응, 그녀는 지난달에 수상스키를 탔어.

➡ Has Sunny tried waterskiing?으로 의문문을 만들고 대답은 3인칭 주어이므로 has로 대답을 한다. 또한 지난 달 (last month)은 과거이므로 try의 과거인 tried를 써서 문장을 완성한다.

Oral Test p. 94

1 현재
2 과거 / 현재
3 과거

Progress Test 2 p. 96~98

1 watching 2 raining 3 smoking 4 closing
5 asked / asked 6 knew / known 7 lost / lost
8 wrote / written 9 told(order) us not to talk
10 ordered me to stay in my car 11 visited
12 has lost 13 went 14 have known
15 The work was finished (by him).
16 The newspaper is read by many people.
17 The letter was not written by Jane.
18 Was the accident seen by many people? / it wasn't
19 The window wasn't broken by Nancy.
20 Was the light bulb invented by Thomas Edison? / it was

Unit 09 미래를 나타내는 부사절

Target Words & Review Words p. 93, 108

□ mix ⓥ ~을 섞다	□ job ⓝ 직업
□ go fishing 낚시하러 가다	□ go out 밖으로 나가다
□ cloud ⓝ 구름	□ lose weight 체중이 줄다
□ passport ⓝ 여권	□ take care of ~을 돌보다
□ cold ⓝ 감기	□ airport ⓝ 공항
□ hurry ⓥ 서두르다	□ lock ⓥ 잠그다
□ as soon as ~하자마자	□ medicine ⓝ 약
□ plant ⓝ 식물	□ retire ⓥ 은퇴하다
□ get fat 살찌다	
□ feel better 기분이 나아지다	
□ look for ~을 찾다, 구하다	
□ driver's licence 운전면허증	
□ classical music 클래식 음악	
□ champion ⓝ 우승자, 챔피언	
□ go for a walk 산책하러 나가다	
□ graduate from ~를 졸업하다	

Mini Test p. 102

01 현재
02 현재

Exercise 1 p. 103

1 (1) do (2) did (3) left (4) leaves (5) get (6) get (7) stops (8) don't eat (9) rains (10) is (11) arrives (12) went (13) see (14) lie (15) go

Exercise 2 p. 104

1 (1) is playing tennis on Saturday
(2) is having dinner with Bob
(3) is going to the movies tonight
(4) are going to a party
2 (1) take (2) works (3) win (4) rains

Exercise 3 p.105

1 (1) travel to Korea / will meet some nice people
(2) water the plants / won't die
(3) goes to bed / will listen to classical music

Jump up! p.106

1 (1) When I retire, I will play tennis.
(2) When I'm old, I will take care of myself.
(3) After he finishes / he's going to go to bed
(4) Before Ann watches / she will finish
(5) When I call / I will ask him to come
(6) Kelly's going to read / after she gets
(7) When Sunny graduates she will look for
(8) When I am 25 years old, I will get

1 (1) 내가 은퇴했을 때, 나는 테니스를 칠 것이다.
⇒ 시간의 부사절 안에 동사는 현재(retire)를 써서 미래를 나타내야 한다. 따라서 When I retire, I will play tennis.로 문장을 완성한다.
(2) 내가 나이가 들었을 때, 나는 내 자신을 돌볼 것이다.
⇒ 시간의 부사절 안에 현재 동사를 써서 미래를 표현한다. 따라서 When I am old, I will ~로 문장을 완성한다.
(3) 그의 숙제를 끝낸 후에, 그는 잠을 자러 갈 것이다.
⇒ 시간의 부사절 안에 또한 현재 동사가 미래를 대신한다. 따라서 After he finishes를 써서 표현하고 will finish를 쓰지 않는다. 시간의 부사절과 상관없는 주인절(주인 문장)에는 미래를 나타내는 표현인 will과 be going to 어느 것이든 쓸 수 있다.
(4) Ann은 오늘 밤 TV를 보기 전에, 그녀의 숙제를 끝낼 것이다.
⇒ 시간의 부사절 안에도 현재 시제로 미래를 표현한다. 따라서 Before Ann watches ~로 표현하고 will watch로 쓰지 않는다.
(5) 내가 내일 Bob에게 전화를 할때, 나는 그에게 내 파티에 오라고 요청할 것이다.
⇒ 시간의 부사절이므로 When I call ~의 현재 시제로 미래를 표현한다.
(6) Kelly는 오늘 밤 집에 도착한 후에 역사책을 읽을 것이다.
⇒ 시간의 부사절이므로 after she gets~로 영작하고 주인 문장(주절)에는 미래 시제 be going to를 그대로 써 준다.
(7) Sunny가 졸업할 때, 그녀는 직업을 구할 것이다.
⇒ 시간의 부사절 when 안에 현재 동사 graduates가 미래를 표현한다.
(8) 내가 25살이 될 때, 나는 결혼을 할 것이다.
⇒ 시간의 부사절 안에서는 현재동사 am이 미래를 표현한다.

Writing Activity p.107

1 (1) does / begin / begins (2) opens (3) leaves
2 (1) If you go out without a coat, you'll get a cold.
(2) If you don't eat breakfast, you will be hungry.
(3) If you eat too many chocolates, you will get fat.
(4) If you go to bed early, you won't be tired the next day.

1 (1) A: 내일 아침에 수업이 몇 시에 시작하니?
B: 7시에 시작해.
⇒ 정해진 일정이나 시간표에는 현재 시제가 미래를 대신한다. What time does the class begin ~?으로 의문문을 만들고 It begins ~로 대답을 한다.
(2) 그 극장은 내일 아침 7시에 문을 연다. 나는 8시에 거기에서 Kathy를 만날 것이다.
⇒ 정해진 일정은 현재 시제가 미래를 대신한다. 주어가 3인칭 단수이므로 opens를 쓴다.

(3) A: 오늘밤 몇 시에 서울역에 갈 예정이니?
B: Bob의 열차는 7시 30분쯤에 떠날 거야, 그런데 나는 조금 더 일찍 갈 생각이야.
➡ 기차표와 같이 정해진 시간에는 현재 시제가 미래를 대신하므로 leaves를 써서 문장을 완성한다.

2 (1) 만약 네가 코트를 입지 않고 밖으로 나가면, 너는 감기에 걸릴 것이다.
➡ 조건의 부사절 안에서도 현재 시제가 미래를 대신하므로 If you go out ~으로 문장을 완성한다. 주절에는 미래를 나타내는 will과 be going to를 써야 하므로 you will get a cold를 써서 영작한다.

(2) 네가 아침을 먹지 않으면, 너는 배고플 거야.
➡ 마찬가지로 조건의 부사절이므로 If you don't eat~을 써서 문장을 완성하고 부정문 won't를 쓰지 않는 것에 주의하자.

(3) 네가 초콜릿을 너무 많이 먹으면, 너는 살이 찔 거야.
➡ 조건의 부사절에는 현재 시제로 If you eat too many chocolates, 주절에는 미래 시제를 써서 문장을 완성한다.

(4) 일찍 잠자리에 들면, 너는 다음날 피곤하지 않을 거야.
➡ 주절에는 미래 시제를 써서 표현해야 하므로 미래시제의 부정문인 won't be tired ~로 문장을 완성한다.

Oral Test p. 108

1 현재 / will/be going to
2 현재 / 미래
3 현재 / 현재진행형

Unit 10 관계대명사 1

Target Words & Review Words p. 109, 118

- □ dentist ⓝ 치과의사
- □ healthy ⓐ 건강한
- □ saw ⓝ 톱
- □ attract ⓥ 끌다, 매혹하다
- □ research ⓝ 연구, 조사
- □ star in (영화에)주연하다
- □ painter ⓝ 화가
- □ worth ⓐ 가치가 있는
- □ apply ⓥ 지원하다
- □ injure ⓥ 다치게 하다
- □ uncle ⓝ 삼촌
- □ tourist ⓝ 관광객, 여행자
- □ special ⓐ 특별한, 특이한
- □ popular ⓐ 인기 있는
- □ biography ⓝ 전기, 일대기
- □ navigation ⓝ 항해, 비행, 항공
- □ be covered with …로 덮혀 있다
- □ be interested in …에 관심이 있다
- □ friendly ⓐ 친절한
- □ climb ⓥ …을 기어 오르다
- □ direction ⓝ 방향, 위치
- □ lay ⓥ (알을) 낳다
- □ animal ⓝ 동물
- □ huge ⓐ 거대한, 매우 큰
- □ next door 옆집에 (사는)
- □ fresh ⓐ 신선한
- □ ending ⓝ 결말, 끝
- □ tool ⓝ 도구
- □ every half hour 30분마다
- □ scientific ⓐ 과학(적인)의
- □ ostrich ⓝ 타조
- □ statue ⓝ 조각상

Mini Test p. 112

01 대명사
02 사람 / 동물 / 사물
03 주어(명사)
04 단수 / 복수

Exercise 1 p. 113

1 (1) who (2) which (3) who (4) who (5) which (6) who (7) which (8) which (9) who (10) which (11) who (12) who (13) which (14) who (15) who

Exercise 2 p. 114

1 (1) were (2) is (3) has (4) is (5) lives (6) tells (7) were (8) works (9) live
2 (1) who live in Seoul (2) who gave me directions
(3) which runs every half hour
(4) which have many windows

Exercise 3 p.115

1 (1) who / lives (2) which / attracts
(3) who / has (4) who / loves (5) which / sleeps
(6) which / lay (7) who / talks

2 (1) who does some scientific research
(2) which makes honey

Jump up! p.116

1 (1) Australia is a country which has some special animals.
(2) Kangaroos are animals which live in Australia.
(3) An ostrich is a bird which doesn't fly.
(4) An orange is a fruit which has a lot of vitamin C.
(5) Do you know the man who took care of animals in his life?
(6) The Beatles were four young men who became famous all over the world.
(7) Brad Pitt is an actor who stars in a lot of popular movies.
(8) James Dean was an actor who died young.
(9) The Sphinx is a huge statue which is near the pyramids.

1 (1) 호주는 하나의 나라이다. 그것은 특별한 동물을 가지고 있다. → 호주는 특별한 동물을 가지고 있는 하나의 나라이다.
➡ a country와 It이 같은 명사이다. 따라서 It을 대명사 which 또는 that으로 바꿔 a country 뒤에 그대로 써 주면 된다. 이때 선행사인 a country가 사람이 아니므로 관계대명사 which 또는 that을 사용한다.

(2) 캥거루는 동물이다. 그들은 호주에 산다. → 캥거루는 호주에 살고 있는 동물이다.
➡ animals와 They가 같은 명사이다. 따라서 They를 관계대명사 which 또는 that으로 바꿔 선행사 animals 뒤에 모두 써주면 된다. 이때 선행사가 동물이므로 which나 that을 쓴다.

(3) 타조는 새이다. 그것은 날지 못한다. → 타조는 날지 못하는 새이다.
➡ a bird와 It이 같은 명사이다. 선행사가 동물(a bird)이므로 It을 which 또는 that으로 바꿔 선행사 뒤에 모두 써 주면 된다.

(4) 오렌지는 과일이다. 그것은 많은 비타민 C를 가지고 있다. → 오렌지는 많은 비타민 C를 가지고 있는 과일이다.
➡ a fruit와 It이 같은 명사이다. It을 대명사 which 또는 that으로 써서 선행사 a fruit 뒤에 모두 써 주면 된다.

(5) 그 남자를 아십니까? 그는 살아오면서 동물들을 돌보았습니다. → 살아오면서 동물들을 돌본 그 남자를 아십니까?
➡ the man과 He는 같은 명사이다. 사람이므로 He를 관계대명사 who로 고쳐 선행사 the man 뒤에 모두 써 주면 된다. 물론 관계대명사 that을 써도 된다.

(6) 비틀즈는 네 명의 젊은 남자들이였다. 이 젊은 남자들은 전 세계에서 유명한 사람이 되었다. → 비틀즈는 전 세계에서 유명한 사람이 된 네 명의 젊은 남자들이였다.
➡ four young men과 These young men이 같은 명사이다. 따라서 These young men을 대명사 who(that)로 고쳐 선행사 four young men 뒤에 써 주면 된다.

(7) Brad Pitt는 배우이다. 이 배우는 많은 인기 있는 영화에서 주연을 맡았다. → Brad Pitt는 많은 인기 있는 영화에서 주연을 맡은 배우이다.
➡ an actor와 This actor가 공통 명사이다. 따라서 This actor를 대명사 who(that)으로 바꿔 선행사 an actor 뒤에 써 주면 된다.

(8) James Dean은 배우였다. 이 배우는 젊은 나이에 죽었다. → James Dean은 젊은 나이에 죽은 배우이다.
➡ an actor와 This actor가 공통 명사이다. 따라서

This actor를 대명사 Who(that)으로 바꿔 선행사 an actor 뒤에 써 주면 된다.

(9) 스핑크스는 큰 동상이다. 그것은 피라미드 가까이에 있다. → 스핑크스는 피라미드 가까이에 있는 큰 동상이다.

➡ a huge statue와 It이 동일한 명사이다. 따라서 It을 which(that)으로 바꿔 선행사인 a huge statue 뒤에 붙여 그대로 써 주면 된다.

Writing Activity p.117

1 (1) who draws pictures
(2) which helps you find your way
(3) who saves people's lives
(4) which won the Champions League last year

2 (1) 화가는 그림을 그리는 사람이다.

➡ who는 선행사가 사람일 때, which는 선행사가 사물/동물일 때 쓴다. 선행사가 사람이므로 who를 쓰고, 주어를 대신하는 관계대명사이므로 주어 없이 draws pictures를 연이어 써 주면 된다.

(2) 네비게이션은 당신이 길을 잃을 때 길을 찾도록 도와주는 것이다.

➡ 선행사가 something이므로 which를 쓴다. 주격 관계대명사이므로 주어 없이 helps you find your way를 연이어 써준다. 관계대명사의 단수/복수는 선행사에 의해 결정된다. 선행사 something이 단수이므로 동사 help또한 단수 동사를 써야 한다.

(3) 소방관은 사람들의 생명을 구하는 사람이다.

➡ 선행사가 사람이므로 who를 쓴다. 선행사가 단수 이므로 saves people's lives로 동사 save를 단수 동사로 써야 한다.

(4) 맨체스터 유나이티드는 작년에 챔피언스 리그를 우승한 축구팀이다.

➡ 선행사가 the soccer team 이므로 관계 대명사 which를 쓴다. 작년이라는 명확한 과거 표시어구 last year가 있으므로 동사 win은 과거인 won으로 써서 영작해야 한다.

Oral Test p.118

1 대명사 / 문장 / 문장 2 who / which / that
3 주격 4 단수 / 복수

Unit 11 관계대명사 2

Target Words & Review Words p.119, 128

- funny ⓐ 우스운, 웃기는
- shocking ⓐ 충격적인
- farm ⓝ 농장, 농원
- draw ⓥ (그림을) 그리다
- cancel ⓥ 취소하다
- honesty ⓝ 정직
- magician ⓝ 마술사
- hat ⓝ 모자
- perfect ⓐ 완벽한
- touching ⓐ 감동적인
- fantastic ⓐ 환상적인, 멋진
- happen ⓥ 생기다, 일어나다
- attend ⓥ (학교 등에) 다니다
- unfortunately ⓥ 믿다, 신뢰하다
- steal ⓥ 훔치다
- movie star 영화배우
- relax ⓥ 쉬다
- voice ⓝ 목소리
- hate ⓥ 싫어하다
- fit ⓥ 어울리다
- own ⓥ 소유하다
- magazine ⓝ 잡지
- visit ⓥ 방문하다

Mini Test p.122

01 1 사람 / 목적어 2 사물 / 동물 / 목적어
02 whose
03 선행사 / 명사

Exercise 1 p.123

1 (1) that (2) which (3) whose (4) that (5) which
(6) whose (7) who (8) What (9) whose
(10) what (11) who (12) which (13) which
(14) what (15) whose

Exercise 2
p.124

1 (1) whom (2) who (3) whom (4) who (5) whom (6) whom (7) who (8) whom (9) who

Exercise 3
p.125

1 (1) X (2) X (3) who(that) (4) who(that) (5) X
2 (1) whose brother is a soccer player
(2) whose dream is to go to Korea
(3) whose puppy died

Jump up!
p.126

1 (1) My girlfriend gave me what I wanted.
(2) He'll do what he can do for her.
2 (1) ②, ③ (2) ③ (3) ①, ②, ④
3 ⑤

1 (1) 내 여자 친구는 나에게 그것을 주었다. 나는 그것을 원했다. → 내 여자 친구는 내가 원한 것을 주었다.
➡ what은 선행사 없이 단독으로 관계대명사 역할을 한다. the thing which를 한 단어 what으로 표현 하므로 what(=the thing which) I wanted으로 고쳐 문장을 완성한다.
(2) 그는 어떤 것도 할 것이다. 그는 그녀를 위해 그것을 할 수 있다. → 그는 그녀를 위해 할 수 있는 것을 할 것이다.
➡ 선행사를 포함하는 what을 이용해 what he can do for her로 문장을 만들어 He'll do what he can do for her.로 문장을 완성한다. 이때의 what은 anything that과 같다.

2 (1) 우리는 지난밤에 봤던 그 영화를 정말로 즐겼다.
➡ we saw 뒤에 '~를 보다'라는 목적어가 없는 것을 보고 목적격 관계대명사임을 알 수 있다. 따라서 선행사가 the movie이므로 which나 that을 쓴다. 또는, 일상영어에서 목적격 관계대명사는 언제나 생략해서 쓸 수 있다.
(2) 나는 누군가의 아름다운 목소리를 들었다.
➡ 빈칸 뒤에 명사 voice가 있기 때문에 소유격 관계대명사인 것을 알 수 있다. 목적격 관계대명사도 '주어+동사'로 이어 질 수 있지만 voice is beautiful처럼 목적어를 대신 한 것이 아니므로 소유격 관계대명사를 써야 한다. 여기서 whose는 someone's voice이다.
(3) 내가 비행기에서 읽었던 그 잡지는 재미있었다.
➡ 빈칸 뒤에 I read를 보면 read의 목적어가 없다. 따라서 목적격 관계대명사임을 쉽게 알 수 있다. 선행사가 사물이므로 which나 that 또는 언제나 생략할 수 있다.

3 ➡ 선행사 없이 두 문장을 연결시킬 수 있는 것은 what밖에 없다.

Writing Activity
p.127

1 (1) Have you found the books which(that) you lost?
(2) I like the dress which(that) Sunny is wearing.
(3) The airplane which(that) I took to Nigeria was on time.
(4) The teacher who(that) was ill canceled her English class.
(5) Those are the girls whose Korean is almost perfect.
2 (1) Albert Einstein was a boy. / He hated school.
(2) The people were Korean. / Nancy visited them yesterday.
(3) The strange woman was a ghost. / We saw her at the park last night.

1 (1) 책들을 찾았나요? 당신은 그 책들을 잃어버렸다. → 잃어버린 책들을 찾았나요?
➡ 양쪽 문장의 the books가 공통 명사이다. 뒤에 있는 the books를 which나 that으로 바꿔 선행사 뒤로 관계대명사를 옮기고 나머지는 그대로 써주면 된다. 목적어를 대명사처리 했으므로 목적격 관계대명사가 된다.

(2) 나는 그 옷을 좋아한다. Sunny는 옷을 입고 있다. → 나는 Sunny가 입고 있는 옷을 좋아한다.

➡ the dress와 a dress가 공통 명사이다. 선행사가 사물이므로 뒤에 나온 명사를 which나 that으로 바꿔 문장을 연결한다. 목적격 관계대명사가 된다.

(3) 그 비행기는 시간에 맞게 도착했다. 나는 나이지리아로 가는 비행기를 탔다. → 나이지리아로 가는 내가 탄 비행기는 시간에 맞게 도착했다.

➡ The airplane과 the airplane이 공통명사이다. 선행사가 사물이므로 which 또는 that으로 바꿔 문장을 완성하면 된다. take의 목적어인 the airplane을 대명사 처리 했으므로 목적격 관계대명사가 된다.

(4) 선생님은 그녀의 영어수업을 취소했다. 선생님은 편찮았다. → 편찮은 선생님은 그녀의 영어 수업을 취소했다.

➡ 양쪽 문장의 The teacher가 공통 명사이다. 주어가 사람이므로 관계대명사 who 또는 that을 이용해 문장을 완성한다. 주어를 대명사 처리했기 때문에 주격 관계대명사가 된다.

(5) 저들이 소녀들이다. 그들의 한국어는 거의 완벽하다. → 저 소녀들의 한국어는 거의 완벽하다.

➡ the girls와 Their이 공통이다. their는 소유격이므로 소유격 관계대명사 whose를 써서 문장을 완성한다.

2 (1) Albert Einstein는 학교를 싫어했던 소년이다.

➡ who는 선행사인 a boy와 공통 명사이다. 따라서 He hated school.로 분리시켜 주면 된다.

(2) Nancy가 어제 방문했던 그 사람들은 한국사람이였다.

➡ whom은 visited의 목적어이다. 따라서 Nancy visited them(the people).로 분리해서 써주면 된다.

(3) 우리가 어젯밤에 공원에서 봤던 그 이상한 여자는 귀신이었다.

➡ that은 saw의 목적어이다. 따라서 We saw her (a strange woman) at the park last night.을 분리해서 써주면 된다.

Oral Test

p.128

1 목적어 / 생략
2 사람 / 사물 / 동물
3 whose
4 what / the thing that(which)

Progress Test 3

p.130~132

1 is 2 who 3 workers 4 makes 5 who loves
6 If it rains tomorrow
7 If Seo-yoon[she] has enough time
8 If they don't study tonight 9 which 10 whose
11 who 12 what
13 who(that) cooks food in the restaurants
14 who(that) fixes old cars
15 who(that) takes pictures
16 who(that) takes care of the sick people
17 When I retire, I will play golf.
18 After Nancy finishes her homework, she's going to watch TV tonight.
19 Before Kelly goes to bed, she's going to finish her work.
20 When we call Peter tomorrow, we'll ask him to our party.

Final Test

p.134~140

1 to show 2 to wish 3 to ask 4 to have 5 ②
6 reading a newspaper
7 painted by a famous artist
8 injured in the traffic accident 9 ⑤ 10 ④
11 whose 12 which 13 ⑤
14 This parcel will be sent (by him)
15 This museum was designed
16 The Great Wall in China was built 17 ③
18 ④ 19 ① 20 I have lost my key.
21 Kevin has gone to Singapore.
22 I am too weak to move the heavy box.
23 She was too sleepy to finish her homework.

24 Michael is too tired to go out tonight.
25 Sunny is strong enough to carry the refrigerator.
26 I had enough time to watch a movie last week.
27 Do you have enough money to buy a new car?
28 destroyed the house / was destroyed by the fire
29 organized a summer trip / was organized by the students
30 cooked dinner / was cooked by my mom
31 directed "Star Wars" / was directed by George Lucas 32 have known / was
33 has had / came 34 moved / got
35 for / since 36 for 37 since 38 since
39 I wrote a letter to the woman. / I met her at the meeting.
40 The pianist who(that) played at the concert last night is internationally famous.

I can Grammar 4

Workbook

I can Grammar 4

Workbook

Unit 01 Basic Workbook

1 주어진 단어를 이용하여 현재완료형의 문장을 완성하세요.

(1) I ________________ to Singapore twice. (be)

(2) We ________________ in this house. (live)

(3) She ________________ all over the world. (travel)

(4) Karen ________________ a lot of interesting people. (meet)

(5) Nancy ________________ a lot of interesting things. (do)

(6) Kelly ________________ married three times. (be)

(7) The writer ________________ ten books. (write)

2 다음 두 문장이 같은 뜻이 되도록 알맞은 표현을 빈칸에 쓰세요.

(1) Kelly went to China, so she is not here.
➡ Kelly ________________ to China.

(2) Mary isn't here. She went home.
➡ Mary ________________ home.

(3) I lost my wallet, and I don't find it now.
➡ I ________________ my wallet.

(4) Kevin is not going to the party. He broke his arm.
➡ Kevin ________________ his arm.

(5) Linda and Nancy don't live here anymore. They moved to Seoul.
➡ Linda and Nancy ________________ to Seoul.

Unit 01 Practice Workbook

1 다음 상황에 맞도록 주어진 표현을 이용해서 의문문과 그 대답을 완성하세요.

(1)

They / buy / new computers
→ No / cellphones

______________________________?

➡ No, ________________.

They ______________________.

(2)

Jenny / buy / a new cellphone
→ No / a new digital camera

______________________________?

➡ No, ________________.

She ______________________.

2 Peter가 경험한 일이 체크되어 있는 아래의 리스트를 참고하여 완료시제 또는 완료시제 부정문을 완성하세요.

Exciting things to do

(1) try scuba diving ✓
(2) travel around Australia
(3) taste snakes
(4) stay in the jungle for a week ✓

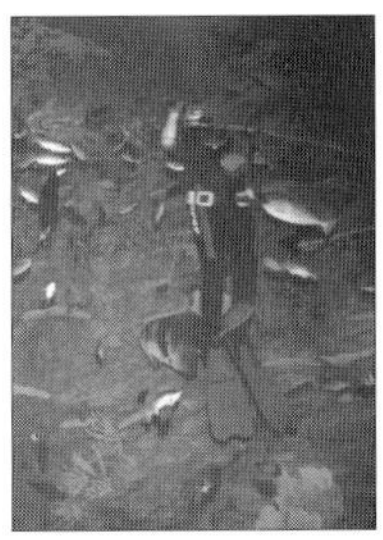

(1) Peter ________ already ______________________.

(2) Peter ______________________________ yet.

(3) Peter ______________________________ yet.

(4) Peter ________ already ______________________.

unit 02 Basic Workbook

( ) 안에 알맞은 분사의 형태를 고르세요.

(1) The puppy is (following / followed) the man.

(2) Look at the (running / run) people.

(3) This soccer game is very (exciting / excited).

(4) The movie was very (boring / bored).

(5) Do you know the woman (wearing / worn) a hat?

(6) Watch out the (breaking / broken) glasses!

(7) It's a house (building / built) years ago.

(8) This is a car (making / made) in China.

(9) A beautiful girl is (smiling / smiled) at me.

(10) He is an (interesting / interested) person.

(11) Look at the (sleeping / slept) tiger!

(12) We saw the ghost (jumping / jumped) over the fence.

(13) Who is the man (waiting / waited) for you at the door?

(14) Is this the letter (writing / written) by Kelly?

(15) This is the thief (arresting / arrested) by the police officer.

Unit 02 Practice Workbook

1 빈칸에 알맞은 분사를 넣어 문장을 완성하세요.

보기

exciting	boring	fascinating	surprised
excited	shocked	interested	

(1) I'm very ____________ because we're going to Seattle next week.

(2) This was a very ____________ book.

(3) I was ____________ by the ending of the story.

(4) I read the book quickly because it was so ____________.

(5) They like swimming, but they're not ____________ in jogging.

(6) We didn't enjoy the movie very much. It was too ____________.

(7) The whole building was on fire. We were all ____________.

2 빈칸에 알맞은 말을 보기 에서 골라 알맞은 형태로 고쳐 쓰세요.

보기

prepare dinner in the kitchen   please with my birthday present   hold a cellphone

(1) 

The man ____________________________ is my brother.

(2) 

The woman ____________________________ is my mom.

(3) 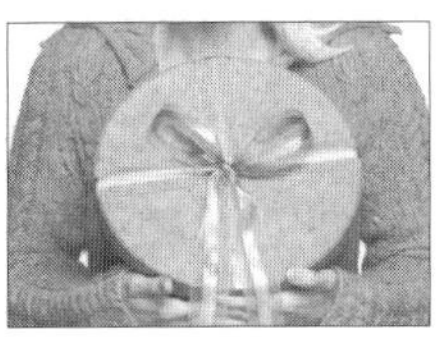

She was very ____________________________.

Unit 03 Basic Workbook

1 to 또는 for를 이용하여 문장을 완성해 보세요.

(1) I went to Singapore ____________ a visit.

(2) I went to Singapore ____________ visit my uncle and aunt.

(3) We wear coats in the winter ____________ keep warm.

(4) We wear coats in the winter ____________ warmth.

(5) Albert went to the store ____________ buy some bread.

(6) We went to a restaurant ____________ have dinner.

(7) He wants to go to college ____________ study economics.

(8) I'm going to Seattle ____________ an interview next week.

(9) I play tennis twice a week ____________ exercises and relaxation.

2 too 또는 enough를 넣어 문장을 완성하세요.

(1) The country is rich ____________ to take care of homeless people.

(2) Eric is ____________ weak to lift that light box.

(3) Justin is ____________ full to eat another hamburger.

(4) Karen is kind ____________ to help others.

(5) Nancy was ____________ sick to do the homework.

(6) Jason is tall ____________ to reach the ceiling.

unit 03 Practice Workbook

1 아래의 내용은 Sunny가 어제 한 일입니다. 오른쪽에 있는 것 중 뜻이 통하는 부분의 기호를 왼쪽 밑줄에 쓰고, 6가지 일에 대한 목적을 나타내는 to 부정사를 활용하여 Sunny를 주어로 하는 문장을 영작하세요.

f	(1)	turn on / the TV	a. make / a cake
____	(2)	go / to the post office	b. borrow / a book
____	(3)	go / to the library	c. invite / her to a party
____	(4)	buy / a magazine	d. buy / stamps
____	(5)	send / e-mail / to Linda	e. read / an article / about her favorite pop star
____	(6)	buy / flour and sugar	f. watch / the news

(1) Sunny turned on the TV to watch the news.

(2) ______________________________.

(3) ______________________________.

(4) ______________________________.

(5) ______________________________.

(6) ______________________________.

2 주어진 단어를 활용하여 문장을 완성하세요.

(1)

(was surprised / get / an unexpected gift)

Our mom ______________________

______________________.

(2)

(was too tired / go out tonight)

Susan ______________________.

Basic Workbook

1 빈칸에 for 또는 since를 쓰세요.

(1) Bob and Alice have been married __________ 20 years.

(2) My uncle has lived in Australia __________ 15 years.

(3) Kelly is in her office. She has been there __________ 6 o'clock.

(4) Now Mark is at the school gym. He has been there __________ 9:00 this morning.

(5) It has been so cold __________ last week.

(6) They have watched the soccer game __________ three hours.

(7) Nick and Peter have been in the same class __________ many years.

(8) Mexico has been an independent country __________ 1821.

(9) Nobody lives in those houses. They have been empty __________ many years.

2 다음 주어진 단어를 이용하여 우리말에 맞게 빈칸을 완성하세요.

(1) 그들은 5년 동안 그곳에서 일해 왔다. (work, there, for 5 years)

➡ They ______________________________________.

(2) 서울에 얼마나 오랫동안 사셨나요? (live, you, in Seoul)

➡ How long ______________________________________?

(3) Justin은 2005년부터 고등학교에서 영어를 가르치고 있다.

(teach, English, in high school, since 2005)

➡ Justin ______________________________________.

(4) Susan과 Nancy는 4년 전에 대학에서 처음 만났다.

그들은 4년 동안 친구로 지내고 있다. (be, friends, for four years)

➡ Susan and Nancy first met at the university four years ago.

They ______________________________________.

| 다음 그림을 보고 보기 에 주어진 단어들을 적절히 활용하여 문장을 영작하세요.

보기
two hours   forty minutes   seven   for   since
play computer games / clean the house / prepare breakfast / date

(1) 

My dad ______________________________
______________________________.

(2) 

Ron and Tom ______________________________
______________________________.

(3) 

Jason and Lisa ______________________________
______________________________.

(4) 

Linda and Kevin ______________________________
______________________________.

unit 05 Basic Workbook

1 빈칸에 to 또는 for를 쓰세요.

(1) A teacher gave questions ________ the students.

(2) A waiter shows the menu ________ you in a restaurant.

(3) Jason wrote a poem ________ her.

(4) I will buy a computer ________ her.

(5) My dad made a new bed ________ me.

2 보기 와 같이 (　) 안의 형용사를 이용하여 질문에 대한 답을 쓰세요.

보기
How do you feel today?
➡ I feel happy. (happy)

(1) 

How does the cake taste?

➡ ____________________. (good)

(2) 

How do I look in this dress?

➡ ____________________. (beautiful)

(3) 

How do the flowers smell?

➡ ____________________. (sweet)

unit 05 Practice Workbook

1 우리말과 일치하도록 주어진 단어를 활용하여 5형식 문장을 만들어 보세요.

(1) Kelly는 나를 항상 행복하게 만든다. (always, me, Kelly, happy, make)

➡ ____.

(2) 선생님은 우리가 휴식하도록 허락해 주었다. (allow, the teacher, take a break, us)

➡ ____.

(3) 그 영화는 그녀를 대스타로 만들었다. (the movie, her, make, a big star)

➡ ____.

2 Could you ~ please?를 이용하여 보기 와 같이 3형식 의문문을 만들어 보세요.

> 보기
>
> You want to open the door, but your hands are full.
> What do you say to your friend?
> ➡ Could you open the door for me, please ?

(1) Your MP3 player doesn't work. Your friend can repair it. What do you say to your friend?

➡ ____?

(2) Your hands are dirty. The cellphone rings. What do you say to your brother?

➡ ____?

unit 06 Basic Workbook

1 (   ) 안의 동사를 동명사로 만들어서 문장을 다시 쓰세요.

(1) Have they finished (paint) the house?

➡ ____?

(2) Would you mind (close) the window?

➡ ____?

(3) My mom and I will go (shop) this evening.

➡ ____.

(4) Would you like (go) for a walk?

➡ ____?

(5) My brother hates (drink) milk, but he has to because he needs calcium.

➡ ____.

2 다음 지시대로 문장을 완성하세요.

(1) 외국어를 배우는 것은 중요하다. (learn)

➡ ________ a foreign language is important. (동명사)

➡ ________ a foreign language is important. (부정사)

(2) 내 꿈은 의사가 되는 것이다. (become)

➡ My dream is ________ a doctor. (동명사)

➡ My dream is ________ a doctor. (부정사)

(3) Lisa는 그녀의 문제에 관하여 얘기하기 시작했다. (talk)

➡ Lisa started ________ about her problem. (동명사)

➡ Lisa started ________ about her problem. (부정사)

Unit 06 Practice Workbook

1 주어진 표현을 '전치사+동명사'를 이용하여 영작하세요.

보기
Kelly interrupted me. She apologized for that.
➡ Kelly apologized for interrupting me.

(1) I like to watch horror movies. I'm interested in that.
➡ I'm interested ______________ horror movies.

(2) We helped an old woman. She thanked us for that.
➡ An old woman thanked us ______________ her.

(3) Sunny wanted to take a taxi to work. She insisted on that.
➡ Sunny insisted ______________ a taxi.

(4) Bob lost my new cellphone. I forgave him for that.
➡ I forgave Bob ______________ my new cellphone.

(5) I'm not a good art student. I try to draw paintings, but I'm not very good at it.
➡ I'm not good ______________ paintings.

2 주어진 상황에 맞는 문장을 고르세요.

① Would you mind closing the door?
② She hates watching horror movies.
③ She hates eating popcorn.
④ How about wearing these sunglasses?
⑤ She enjoys having dinner with popcorn.

unit 07 Basic Workbook

( ) 안에서 알맞은 단어를 고르세요.

(1) The office (cleaned / is cleaned) every day.

(2) Are these classrooms (cleaned / are cleaned) every day?

(3) This painting (drew / was drawn) by my dad.

(4) He (invited / was invited) them to the party last week.

(5) Farmers (grow / are grown) rice.

(6) Rice (grow / is grown) by farmers.

(7) Lisa (wrote / is written) the letter.

(8) The teacher (explained / was explained) the lesson.

(9) The lesson (explained / was explained) by the teacher.

(10) The telephone (invented / was invented) by Alexander Graham Bell.

(11) These books (wrote / were written) by Shakespeare.

(12) Was the work (finished / was finished) by him?

(13) The washing-up (did / was done) by my sister yesterday.

(14) Mike (introduced / was introduced) his brother to us at the party.

(15) Sunny (likes / is liked) by all her classmates because she always (helps / is helped) her friends when they need her.

Unit 07 Practice Workbook

1 (　　) 안의 단어를 활용하여 수동태 문장을 완성하세요.

(1) 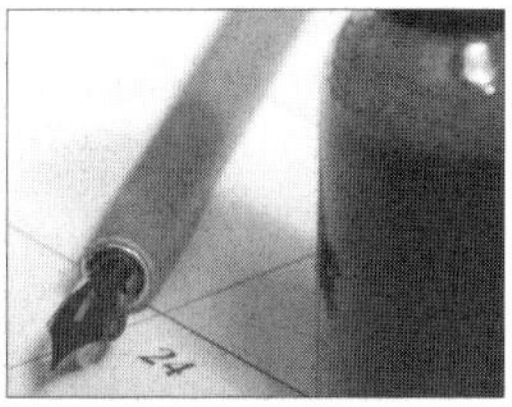

Romeo and Juliet ____________ (write) by Shakespeare.

(2) 

Every year hundreds of people ____________ (kill) in car accidents.

(3) 

These shoes ____________ (make) in Korea.

(4) 

Computer games are very popular, and they ____________ (play) by many teenagers.

2 주어진 문장을 수동태로 바꿔 쓰세요.

(1) Peter doesn't love Kelly.

➡ ____.

(2) Did the students take a math exam?

➡ ____?

(3) The company didn't send e-mails to the customers.

➡ ____.

unit 08 Basic Workbook

1 ( ) 안에서 알맞은 시제를 고르세요.

(1) Emily (visited / has visited) her grandmother last week.

(2) I (lost / have lost) my key. I can't find it.

(3) I (saw / have seen) a ghost yesterday.

(4) My friend is a writer. He (wrote / has written) many books.

(5) We (went / have gone) to the movies, but we didn't enjoy the film much.

(6) She (was / has been) angry because they were late.

(7) Kathy (smoked / has smoked) since university.

(8) Bob (worked / has worked) here since he finished university.

2 주어진 단어를 이용하여 알맞은 과거 또는 현재완료 시제를 쓰세요.

(1) Jason and I are old friends. I __________ (know) him since I __________ (be) a freshman in high school.

(2) Kelly __________ (have) a lot of problems since she __________ (come) to this country.

(3) Nancy __________________ (not / experience) any problems since she __________ (come) here.

(4) Our teacher __________ (give) ten tests since the semester __________ (begin).

(5) Our phone bill __________ (rise) since we __________ (buy) a cellphone.

unit 08 Practice Workbook

우리말과 같은 뜻이 되도록 빈칸을 채우세요.

Kelly	 buy / a gift / for her dad	√	yesterday
Bob	lock / the door	X	
Alice	 fix / her bike	√	on Saturday
Sunny	prepare / breakfast	X	
Our homeroom teacher	give / our homework	X	
My dad	 paint / the house	√	last week
We	 order / pizzas	√	half an hour ago
Lisa	brush / her teeth	X	

보기

Kelly has bought a gift for her dad. She bought it yesterday.
Bob hasn't locked the door.

(1) Alice ______________________________.

(2) Sunny ______________________________.

(3) Our homeroom teacher ______________________________.

(4) My dad ______________________________.

(5) We ______________________________.

(6) Lisa ______________________________.

unit 09 Basic Workbook

1 주어진 문장을 하나로 합칠 때, ( ) 안에 알맞은 시제를 고르세요.

(1) Karen and Justin will get married. Then Karen will graduate.
➡ Karen and Justin (will get / get) married before Karen (will graduate / graduates).

(2) I'll lend Lisa some money. She needs it.
➡ I (will lend / lend) Lisa some money if she (will need / needs) it.

(3) They will win the game. They will be champions.
➡ If they (will win / win) the game, they (will be / are) champions.

2 다음 주어진 정보를 이용하여 현재진행형 시제로 미래를 표현해 보세요.

(1)

play soccer / on Sunday

Tom ______________________.

(2)

go to the movies / tonight

They ______________________.

(3)

have a party / next weekend

Laura ______________________.

(4)
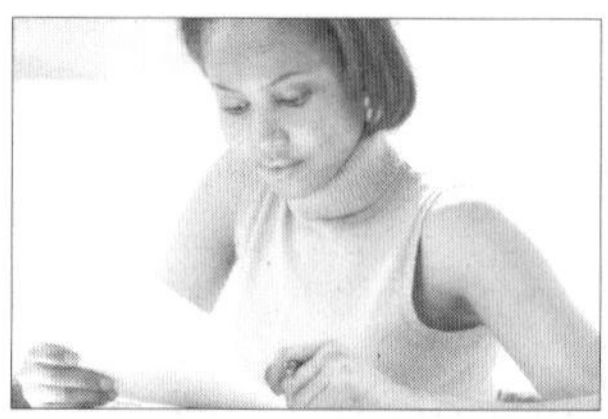
take an English course / this semester

Nancy ______________________
______________________.

Unit 09 Practice Workbook

1 조건의 부사절에는 현재시제를 그리고 주절(주인 문장)에는 미래 시제를 나타내는 조동사 will을 써서 문장을 완성하세요.

(1) What are we doing this Sunday? Well, if the weather ________ (be) nice, we ________ ________ (go) to the Lotte World.

(2) If it __________ (rain), we ________________ (stay) at home.

(3) If we __________ (stay) at home, we ________________ (watch) TV.

(4) We ________________ (watch) a movie if there ________ (be) nothing good on TV.

2 주어진 문장을 읽고, 조건의 부사절을 이용하여 문장을 완성하세요.

(1) 

Bob must run very fast, and he will win the race.

➡ ____.

(2) 

The dress may be expensive, so Linda may not buy it.

➡ ____.

(3) 

Unless you take a subway, you will be late for work.

➡ ____.

Unit 10 Basic Workbook

1 ( ) 안에서 알맞은 말을 고르세요.

(1) The woman (who / which) answered the phone was polite.

(2) He (who / which) loses health loses everything.

(3) There are many buildings (who / which) were built two hundred years ago.

(4) This is the tiger (who / which) bit me.

(5) I don't like movies (who / which) are full of special effects.

(6) I love that girl (who / which) is sitting on the bench.

2 주어진 문장을 보기 와 같이 두 문장으로 나누어 써 보세요.

보기

The waiter who served us dinner was rude.

➡ The waiter was rude.

➡ He served us dinner.

(1) The river which flows through the city is polluted.

➡ ______________________ polluted.

➡ ______________________ through the city.

(2) An old woman who was wearing a big hat asked me for directions.

➡ ______________________ me for directions.

➡ ______________________ a big hat.

(3) The professor had an assistant who did everything for him.

➡ ______________________ an assistant.

➡ ______________________ for him.

주어진 표현을 관계대명사를 이용하여 한 문장으로 만드세요.

(1) 

A photographer is someone / takes pictures

➡ ______________________________

______________________________.

(2) 

Neil Armstrong was the first man / walked on the moon

➡ ______________________________

______________________________.

(3) 

That is the lifeguard / saved my life

➡ ______________________________

______________________________.

(4) 

I met a woman last night. / was really beautiful

➡ ______________________________

______________________________.

(5) 

You must get the vitamins / are important to your health

➡ ______________________________

______________________________.

unit 11 Basic Workbook

1 (　　) 안에서 알맞은 관계대명사를 고르세요.

(1) My English teacher is the man (whose / what / who) I'll never forget.

(2) I know the woman (whose / that / which) house is by the river.

(3) I gave her the book (which / who / what) she wanted.

(4) Here is the key (which / what / whose) you are looking for.

(5) I saw an old castle (who / whose / which) stood on the hill.

(6) I want to give you (who / which / what) you need.

(7) She is the best cook (that / which / whose) I have ever met.

(8) Jane is my friend (who / whose / what) hair is black.

2 두 문장을 관계대명사 whose를 사용하여 한 문장으로 만드세요.

(1) We have the mountain. Its top is covered with snow.

➡ We have the mountain ______________________________.

(2) I met a man. His wife is an English teacher.

➡ I met a man ______________________________.

(3) We met a girl. Her beauty took our breath away.

➡ We met a girl ______________________________.

Unit 11 Practice Workbook

주어진 표현을 관계대명사 which나 what을 이용하여 한 문장으로 만드세요.

(1) 

The thing was shocking. / We saw the thing.

➡ ______________________________
______________________________.

(2) 

The picture is very interesting. / She drew the picture.

➡ ______________________________
______________________________.

(3) 

The plane arrived on time. / I took the plane to Korea.

➡ ______________________________
______________________________.

(4) 

We are polluting the water and air. All life needs the water and air.

➡ ______________________________
______________________________.

정답 및 해설

unit 01 현재완료

Basic Workbook p. 2

1 (1) have been (2) have lived (3) has traveled
(4) has met (5) has done (6) has been
(7) has written

2 (1) has gone (2) has gone (3) have lost
(4) has broken (5) have moved

Practice Workbook p. 3

1 (1) Have they bought new computers? /
they haven't /
have bought new cellphones
(2) Has Jenny bought a new cellphone? /
she hasn't /
has bought a new digital camera

2 (1) has / tried scuba diving
(2) has not traveled around Australia
(3) has not tasted snakes
(4) has / stayed in the jungle for a week

unit 02 현재분사/과거분사

Basic Workbook p.4

1 (1) following (2) running (3) exciting (4) boring
(5) wearing (6) broken (7) built (8) made
(9) smiling (10) interesting (11) sleeping
(12) jumping (13) waiting (14) written (15) arrested

Practice Workbook p. 5

1 (1) excited (2) fascinating (3) surprised
(4) exciting (5) interested (6) boring (7) shocked

2 (1) holding a cellphone
(2) preparing dinner in the kitchen
(3) pleased with my birthday present

unit 03 부사 역할의 부정사

Basic Workbook p. 6

1 (1) for (2) to (3) to (4) for (5) to (6) to (7) to (8) for
(9) for

2 (1) enough (2) too (3) too (4) enough (5) too
(6) enough

Practice Workbook p. 7

1 (2) d / Sunny went to the post office to buy stamps
(3) b / Sunny went to the library to borrow a book
(4) e / Sunny bought a magazine to read an article about her favorite pop star
(5) c / Sunny sent an e-mail to Linda to invite her to a party
(6) a / Sunny bought flour and sugar to make a cake

2 (1) was surprised to get an unexpected gift
(2) was too tired to go out tonight

unit 04 현재완료 계속

Basic Workbook p. 8

1 (1) for (2) for (3) since (4) since (5) since (6) for
(7) for (8) since (9) for

2 (1) have worked there for 5 years
(2) have you lived in Seoul
(3) has taught English in high school since 2005
(4) have been friends for four years

Practice Workbook p. 9

1 (1) has cleaned the house for two hours (for forty minutes / since seven)
(2) have played computer games for two hours (for forty minutes / since seven)
(3) have prepared breakfast for two hours (for forty

minutes / since seven)

(4) have dated for two hours (for forty minutes, since seven)

unit 05 2, 4, 5형식 동사

Basic Workbook p. 10

1 (1) to (2) to (3) to (2) for (2) for

2 (1) It tastes good. (2) You look beautiful.
(3) They smell sweet.

Practice Workbook p. 11

1 (1) Kelly always makes me happy.
(2) The teacher allowed us to take a break.
(3) The movie made her a big star.

2 (1) Could you repair my MP3 player for me, please?
(2) Could you answer the cellphone for me, please?

unit 06 동명사

Basic Workbook p. 12

1 (1) Have they finished painting the house?
(2) Would you mind closing the window?
(3) My mom and I will go shopping this evening.
(4) Would you like going for a walk?
(5) My brother hates drinking milk, but he has to because he needs calcium.

2 (1) Learning / To learn (2) becoming / to become
(3) talking / to talk

Practice Workbook p. 13

1 (1) in watching (2) for helping (3) on taking
(4) for losing (5) at drawing

2 ④

unit 07 수동태

Basic Workbook p. 14

1 (1) is cleaned (2) cleaned (3) was drawn (4) invited
(5) grow (6) is grown (7) wrote (8) explained
(9) was explained (10) was invented (11) were written
(12) finished (13) was done (14) introduced
(15) is liked / helps

Practice Workbook p. 15

1 (1) was written (2) are killed (3) are/were made
(4) are played

2 (1) Kelly isn't loved by Peter.
(2) Was a math exam taken by the students?
(3) E-mails weren't sent to the customers by the company.

unit 08 과거와 현재완료

Basic Workbook p. 16

1 (1) visited (2) have lost (3) saw (4) has written
(5) went (6) was (7) has smoked (8) has worked

2 (1) have known / was (2) has had / came
(3) hasn't experienced / came (4) has given / began
(5) has risen / bought

Practice Workbook p. 17

1 (1) has fixed her bike / She fixed it on Saturday.
(2) hasn't prepared breakfast
(3) hasn't given our homework
(4) has painted the house / He painted it last week.
(5) have ordered pizzas / We ordered them half an hour ago.
(6) hasn't brushed her teeth.

unit 09 미래를 나타내는 부사절

Basic Workbook p. 18

1 (1) will get / graduates (2) will lend / needs
(3) win / will be

2 (1) is playing soccer on Sunday
(2) are going to the movies tonight
(3) is having a party next weekend

(4) is taking an English course this semester

Practice Workbook p. 19

1 (1) is / will go (2) rains / will stay
(3) stay / will watch (4) will watch / is

2 (1) If Bob runs very fast, he will win the race.
(2) If the dress is expensive, Linda may not buy it.
(3) If you don't take a subway, you will be late for work.

unit 10 관계대명사 1

Basic Workbook p. 20

1 (1) who (2) who (3) which (4) which (5) which
(6) who

2 (1) The river is / It flows
(2) An old woman asked / She was wearing
(3) The professor had / The assistant did everything

Practice Workbook p. 21

1 (1) A photographer is someone who[that] takes pictures.
(2) Neil Armstrong was the first man who[that] walked on the moon.
(3) That is the lifeguard who[that] saved my life.
(4) I met a woman last night who[that] was really beautiful.
(5) You must get the vitamins which[that] are important to your health.

unit 11 관계대명사 2

Basic Workbook p. 22

1 (1) who (2) whose (3) which (4) which (5) which
(6) what (7) that (8) whose

2 (1) whose top is covered with snow
(2) whose wife is an English teacher
(3) whose beauty took our breath away

Practice Workbook p. 23

1 (1) What we saw was shocking.
(2) The picture which she drew is very interesting.
(3) The plane which I took to Korea arrived on time.
(4) We are polluting the water and air which all life needs.

I can Grammar

Workbook